BLITZ DIARY

BLITZ DIARY

LIFE UNDER FIRE IN THE SECOND WORLD WAR

**CAROL HARRIS
AND MIKE BROWN**

The
History
Press

First published 2010,
this revised edition published 2020

The History Press
97 St George's Place, Cheltenham,
Gloucestershire, GL50 3QB
www.thehistorypress.co.uk

British Library Cataloguing in Publication Data.
A catalogue record for this book is available from the British Library.

ISBN 978 0 7509 9487 3

Typesetting and origination by The History Press
Printed and bound in Great Britain by TJ International Ltd.

MIX
Paper from
responsible sources
FSC® C013056

CONTENTS

INTRODUCTION

For decades after the end of the Second World War, disused air raid shelters and bomb sites were part of the landscape of towns and cities across the United Kingdom; the twisted frames of derelict factories, terraces of houses whose symmetry ended abruptly in jagged walls exposing fireplaces and peeling wallpaper; buildings that had once been homes, shops, schools and workplaces.

The home front was the main battlefront for the UK in the first half of the war; civilian casualty totals were higher than those for the military until 1942. Bombing was an attempt to terrorise the civil population into submission. The first raids did cause terror, and initially the response of rescue services was chaotic. However, after that initial shock, civilians became hardened by their experiences and more determined to resist and take revenge on the enemy.

Planners on both sides played a game of catch up, regularly changing tactics and targets. This brought more destructive weapons, including high-explosive and incendiary bombs, land mines, delayed action bombs, and the dreaded V-1 flying bomb and V-2 rocket.

In this book, we look at the air assault on Britain through the records and recollections of those who were involved. The accounts tell the story from civilian perspectives – including those in rescue services and the Observer Corps – and from military viewpoints, including the Auxiliary Territorial Service, and those learning on the job in bomb disposal.

Covering the various phases of the assault, it looks at the early attacks on ports; the Big and Little Blitzes; Baedeker, Tip and Run, and Scalded Cat raids, and the final phase of the V-weapons.

These contemporary and first-hand accounts highlight the experiences of those who lived through that time. They are an 'unvarnished truth', in stark contrast to nostalgia, misinformation and period propaganda, which create a mythology that threatens to overwhelm the truth of what happened.

As the generation that fought and endured the Blitz fades away, it is more important than ever that we try to understand how they saw and experienced that time, when ordinary people did and experienced extraordinary things.

Carol Harris and Mike Brown

1

PREPARING FOR WAR

The First World War showed how, in future conflicts, civilian populations would be primary targets. During the 1930s, another European war became increasingly likely. Britain had to look for ways to defend people in towns and cities against bombing and poison gas. Planning focused on civil defence, a term used more and more throughout that decade.

Enemy airships and aeroplanes had dropped bombs on civilian populations across the country during the First World War, killing more than 1,400 people in just over 100 raids. By the standards of the Second World War, these numbers were very low, and the damage, rescue work and injuries could be dealt with by the existing police, fire brigades and ambulance services.

But those planning Britain's defences after the First World War could see how more raids by large groups of aircraft over mainland Britain could mean the difference between victory and defeat in future conflict. In 1924, the British

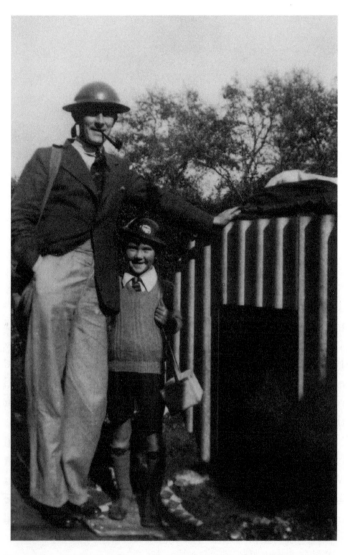

Pictured by the family Anderson shelter, these two still carry their gas
masks, which suggests it is early in the war. Anderson shelters consisted
of curved sheets of aluminium buried several feet in the ground. Earth
was shovelled on the top of the shelter, ideally at a minimum depth of
18in/45cm, for added protection.

government's Committee for Imperial Defence established an Air Raid Precautions (ARP) subcommittee to look at 'the organisation for war, including Civil Defence, home defence, censorship and emergency war legislation'. This subcommittee met secretly for nine years, discussing ways of warning the population of air raids, preventing damage through such measures as restricting lighting (the blackout), gas masks, evacuation, repairing damage and dealing with casualties.

In 1933, the year Hitler became Chancellor of Germany, the subcommittee set out detailed plans for ARP services, which would be organised through local authorities. By 1935, when the ARP Department of the Home Office was set up, these local authorities had been briefed on their responsibilities: the scheme would mean forming services to provide first aid, deal with poison gas attacks and rescue civilians caught in air raids. In that year, Hitler announced that Germany would re-establish her air force and introduce military conscription – both of which were in contravention of the Treaty of Versailles, which had ended the First World War.

The first official radio broadcast on ARP services went out in January 1937 on the BBC. Debate had raged for some time as to the appropriate response to the threat of air raids. Some felt that the introduction of such a scheme was itself provocative. Doctors argued whether they should co-operate at all. Across the country local authorities reflected this ambivalence. Some services were well organised, with volunteers training to deal with the effects; most were not. In general, ARP was regarded as something of a joke.

Attitudes changed markedly in 1937, when cinema newsreels showed the impact of the air raid on the Basque

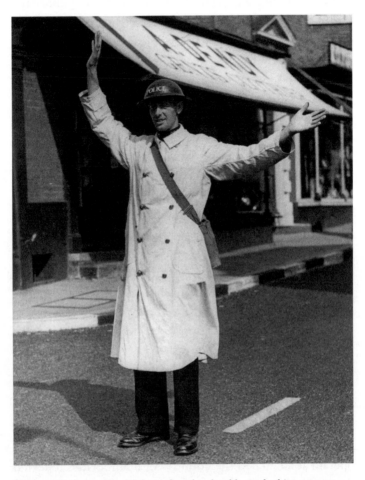

With steel helmet, gas mask hung from his shoulder and white overcoat, this police constable, in September 1939, is ready for war. The painted kerbs, like his coat, are to give added visibility in the blackout.

town of Guernica during the Spanish Civil War. Guernica was attacked on 26 April of that year by German and Italian air forces in support of the fascist or nationalist side. Dr Duncan Leys' letter to the *British Medical Journal*, written a few weeks later, sums up the feelings of many, that Britain was woefully unprepared for the onslaught that was to come:

22nd May 1937

SIR, – It is no longer correct, I find, to think of our work as one of healing. I learn from the Home Office Instructor on Air Raid Precautions in the Birmingham area that my duties in the next war are to aid the police in 'preventing panic,' to 'reassure' the gas casualties, 'to get it into people's heads that whether they have gas-proofed rooms or not the important thing is for them to be under cover in their own houses,' that 'the whole danger of gas attacks lies in the lowering of national morale,' and that the medical profession, as a group of persons 'who can speak with authority,' is to maintain that morale, in which function the Home Office considers them of only less importance than the police.

These actual quotations from a lecture are no misrepresentation of the general tenor. Having heard pacificists [*sic*] maintain that the main object of the Government's air raid precautions scheme was a military one, that is, to make panic or any mass protest against the continuation of war less likely, and that protection from death and injury in air raids on cities was only possible by the erection of bomb-proof shelters which the Government considered too expensive to contemplate – I attended this official lecture, delivered by a doctor to other doctors, on

the invitation of the British Medical Association in order
to learn what attitude was taken by the Home Office
officials themselves. I was prepared to hear the lecturer
say that, with the Prime Minister, he acknowledged that
nothing like protection to a city population was possible
short of bomb-proof and gas-proof shelters constructed
for the purpose, but that until the Government had made
its plans, the possibility of sudden air attack on cities
existed, and that the Air Raid Precautions Department
offered some advice as better than none, that a few lives
might be saved by such advice, and that he was there to
tell us how we could help in this limited sense. Such an
approach to the question would have had my full sympathy and co-operation.

The lecturer opened by assuring us that he had no
connection with the fighting services: the Air Raid
Precautions Department 'had nothing warlike about it,'
and was intended 'purely for the passive protection of
the civil population.' He told us that it would require
anything from a few inches to several feet of concrete
to protect buildings from air raids, and that 'nobody
had suggested that it was possible to protect the whole
population in this way.' He went on to describe how we
might advise people to erect on scaffolding three layers
of filled sandbags on their roofs, with two feet interval
between the layers, to protect them from splinters from
high explosives. No enemy, he continued, would use
gas bombs only; high explosives would first be used to
demolish important centres like railway stations, public
buildings – including hospitals, which would become
too dangerous to be used for other purposes than as
casualty clearing stations – and generally to do as much

damage to structure as possible. Thermite bombs would follow in thousands with the aim of starting a general conflagration in the city beyond the powers of the fire brigades to deal with. Gas would next be sent down by spray or bomb, and it was then that doctors and first-aid services would be needed to 'prevent panic,' to 'reassure' those affected, and to persuade people to remain in their houses.

A passing mention was made of the difficulties of protecting the aged and children and invalids, but respirators 'were a second line of defence' and the main thing was that people should stay indoors. No mention was made of the impossibility for most working-class families of providing a room for gas-proofing (a room rendered uninhabitable because of boarded windows and blocked ventilators or chimney), and although the lecturer said that the modern bombing plane could aim accurately to within seventy-five yards no mention was made of the certainty that windows and gas-proofing would certainly be destroyed over a wide area surrounding the fall of a high-explosive torpedo.

No opportunity was given for questions or discussion, and one is therefore unable to say how far the audience of some thirty doctors accepted the role indicated to them of persuading their neighbours that the Air Raid Precautions Scheme could really save them and their children when it must be perfectly obvious to the meanest intelligence that it can do nothing of the sort, and that the whole apparatus of the scheme is designed to deceive people into thinking that it will. I am not accusing the lecturer of deception: he was painfully honest. It is obviously much more satisfactory, from a military point of view, that people should die quietly in their homes than that they should run about the streets and possibly mob Cabinet Ministers: they might even, fearing retaliation, try to persuade our own airmen from their efforts to destroy French, German, Italian, or Russian cities.

But I should judge that the audience was almost entirely uncritical, accepting war as inevitable and their duty that outlined by the lecturer. The lecturer, by the way, inadvertently said these will be your duties, but corrected himself, and hoped we might avoid seeing the actuality.

I put it to one member of the audience after the lecture that we were being asked to perform a military duty and to help deceive people into thinking that protection was possible on the lines proposed in order that mass protest against war should be made less likely. His reply was that if an enemy attacked us in this way we might as well make it possible for our Air Force to do the same to his cities.

I should personally be sympathetic to any Government which, if it thought that the risk of war could not be avoided, sought power to tax the people to the utmost limit to provide them with protection, putting the facts in an unvarnished way before them and placing the responsibility upon them. But I hold that our people have the democratic right of deciding for themselves, now, in time of peace, whether modern warfare can justify itself, by having none of the facts hidden from them. I call the Government's Air Raid Precautions Scheme wilful deception of the people. I believe also that it is a deception which will defeat its own object. Panic is a mild word for the wrath which the people, rudely enlightened by the first English Guernica, will display against their rulers and officials when they survey the ruins and the dead.

I am, etc.,

DUNCAN LEYS,

M.D.Oxon.

The government realised that massed air raids would stretch the existing emergency services well beyond breaking point, and passed the ARP Act, which came into effect on 1 January 1938. Now local authorities were compelled to set up ARP schemes, and offered substantial funding towards the costs of doing so. Schemes had to include wardens, first aid, gas decontamination, casualty clearing stations and repair and demolition services. The Auxiliary Fire Service, representing a major expansion of the established fire brigades, was also introduced.

Ann Maxtone Graham was the American wife of Pat, a British serviceman, living with their sons at the family home in Earl's Court, London. This is her memoir, written initially to give her family in America an idea of the war in Britain:

Little by little, we started to check what we should do if war came, for we began to believe it might. In March of 1938, Pat enlisted in the 151st battery anti-aircraft brigade and I bought six gallons of gasoline which I stored in a funny little summer house in the back garden. At one time it housed the boys' rabbits. I bought a can of ether in case I had to put the dogs and cats to sleep.

Trenches were dug in Kensington Gardens and Hyde Park and sand bags made protective walls round doorways. Our war didn't burst upon us like Pearl Harbor. It came in sneaky little ways. Suddenly there was a flier in the mail box: 'Notice to inhabitants – Air Raid Precautions.' Gas masks would be issued, they said, 'should it become necessary.'

Pat was away in camp for two week's training and came home on September 26th but was called up the next day, and off he went to his guns and rockets.

In September 1938 Germany occupied the Sudetenland region of Czechoslovakia, and war seemed imminent. Ann volunteered to deliver gas masks to people who could not leave their homes: 'I went flying around, had an hour's training in how to fit the horrid things and then set off on my delivery route.' While she was out on her rounds:

There was a group of people huddled around a wireless and they beckoned me to join them. Mr Chamberlain had just arrived home from Berlin and a conference with Hitler. He was shouting 'Peace in our time! Peace in our time! All is well.' We all collapsed like pricked balloons. After all, he was the Prime Minister, and we thought he knew what he was talking about. I crept home, had my hot bath, but a stiff drink instead of my cup of tea. It had been quite a day. Pat came home from his gun site and went back to his job – there were certain evenings and weekends given to training.

In Britain, the newsreels showed how Prime Minister Neville Chamberlain's attempt to bring 'peace for our time', known as the 'Munich Agreement', was welcomed by cheering crowds. Under the agreement, Hitler assured Chamberlain and the rest of Europe that he had no further territorial demands. In return, Britain and France ignored the Czech government's views and agreed to Germany incorporating the Czech Sudetenland within its own borders. The war that had seemed imminent had been averted. However, across the UK, in the year between Munich and the outbreak of war in September 1939, the numbers of volunteers for the various civil defence services soared. It suggests that few believed the Munich Agreement to be anything more than a delay, in which to prepare as fast as they could for the inevitable conflict. Shelters were dug in public parks; people filled sandbags and buckets of water, and Morrison and Anderson shelters were distributed to civilian homes. Public meetings, volunteer recruitment drives and training schemes for both civil defence personnel and the general public gathered pace. Expectations were that the air raids would start very soon after war was declared, and would result in planes dropping poison gas on the major cities of Britain. Official estimates, based on the effects of bombing in Spain, were that 120,000 people would die in the first week of the war, and about twice that number would be injured. This estimated total of 360,000 casualties in one week was in fact more than twice the number of people killed and injured in Britain in this way during the whole of the war.

Anne Maxtone Graham was typical of those volunteering:

Life went on as usual but there were stirrings, and we felt that maybe someone was doing a little pushing and trying to get ready in case war really came.

It occurred to me that if other people were doing a little pushing, maybe I should do a little quiet pushing too. So I went up to the Town Hall of Kensington, and after a little struggle, I got in to see the man who was in charge of the First Aid Posts.

A group of Auxiliary Ambulance drivers, London, September 1939. The war demanded a huge expansion of the emergency services; women volunteers took on many jobs they had not done in peacetime, including driving ambulances.

As a result, she set up a depot at her home making surgical dressings:

I don't know how many hundreds of thousands of dressings and bandages we made for Kensington, but when they were done they were all dispatched to the Town Hall. To our fury, they were never acknowledged nor did we receive one word of thanks. I know they were used, for some of our friends saw them in the First Aid Posts and recognised my writing on the labels.

So much for Kensington! We supplied Hackney with the things and they were gratefully acknowledged.

The Maxtone Graham family were together for Christmas:

We rented a house in the New Forest for a month at Christmas time (1938). It was right on the Solent opposite the Isle of Wight and all the big ocean liners went past on their way to Southampton. Although we didn't know it, this was our last peaceful Christmas for some very long years, and the last one that I would have with our children. Perhaps there was something that gave us a warning, as we made the most of it, kept the house full of guests, and didn't go back until the 21st January. British children get a month's holiday at Christmas.

My darling Dad died on 23rd March, and I longed to go home to Mother. She had a very nice niece staying with her and she begged me not to come. So I kept on with my surgical dressings and other odd jobs which came my way. A letter from my mother in May asked, 'Aren't you worried about the war? You never mention it, except for the surgical dressings.'

So I broke down and told her about the cans of gasoline stored in the summer house and the ether to put my dogs and cats to sleep if the need arose. No sooner had the letter reached Mother than I had a cable from her to say that she was coming to England at once. And so she did. I don't think she liked the trenches in the park or all the sandbags any better than we did. Nor did she like Pat going off to camp and leaving me all alone in London. She was so distressed about all this that at last I said the boys and I would go back to America with her for a visit. We sailed on July 22nd on the *Georgic*.

That is how I came to be in America when the war started. If I hadn't been there, I would never have sent the boys [Peter aged 12 and twins John and Michael aged 10] to America, as many of my friends and relatives did. But as I was there with them, I had to make a decision as to what I should do. I left them and, sometimes, I wish with all my heart that I had not.

Henry Beckingham, aged 19, had volunteered for military service in May 1939. He had just left technical college and started his first job as a draughtsman with a firm of consulting engineers:

The decision was whether I should go for the TA [Territorial Army], spending weekends in the drill hall plus a 14-day camp annually, or alternatively to wait until the age of 20 years and spend 12 months away with the militia.

I decided that the Territorial Army offered me the best option, as this would not seriously affect my civilian career. How wrong that decision was would be made very clear in the months ahead.

In addition to the call for volunteers to work in military and civilian services, a limited form of conscription was introduced in spring 1939. Under the Military Training Act, single men aged 20–22 were liable to be 'called up' (conscripted). They were to be known as 'militiamen', as they were not part of the regular army. At the outbreak of war the National Service (Armed Forces) Act extended conscription: all fit men between the ages of 18 and 41 could now be compelled to serve in the armed forces.

R.H. Lloyd-Jones was another volunteer. He was a 29-year-old solicitor in Ealing when he joined the Territorial Army in 1938. He served first with the 424 AA (Anti-Aircraft) Company, 36 Searchlight Regiment, RE (Royal Engineers) and here in his memoir, he recalls the work of anti-aircraft, and the reactions of the first batch of conscripts:

Spring and Summer 1939
War was becoming very near and the Government had decided that the Anti-Aircraft defence would have to be permanently manned.

Conscription had come into force and some of the first intake, the militia-men, as they were called, were being trained for AA work, but until they were ready, the existing AA units like our own would have to man the sites, four weeks at a time. This process, quaintly named 'couverture', would start in the middle of June. Our regiment was one of those which were given the second period of four weeks, from 16th July to 14th August 1939 ... At about the same time we were told where our war sites would be. They were dotted over the country every few miles between Bedford and St Neots.

Some of us who had seen the posters 'Join the Anti-Aircraft and defend your homes' had not expected to be so far from our homes. It was explained to us that we would be in the outermost ring of the defences of London.

By now we were being sorted out according to the duties we would be carrying out on site.

Perhaps at this point I should mention that a Searchlight Detachment consisted of ten men who were numbered 1 to 10, these numbers signifying what they had been trained for, no 1 being the Detachment Commander. Nos 2 and 3 were spotters who watched for aircraft with binoculars, or more often with the naked eye because there were not enough binoculars to go round.

No 4 was the Projector Controller who stood or walked at the end of a bracket called the 'long arm' attached to the projector, with a kind of steering wheel to obtain (it was hoped) the right elevation of the beam. No 5 was an electrician, the searchlight operator, responsible for the arc lamp which produced the light. No 6 was in charge of the sound locator and was the Second in Command of the detachment. A one-way telephone enabled him to give directional orders to No 4, who wore a head set for this purpose. Nos 7 and 8 were the listeners who operated the Sound Locator, one of them listening in bearing and the other in elevation. No 9 was in charge of the lorry or diesel generator and No 10 was the spare man, which in actual fact meant that he was the cook.

Our training for these duties was partly individual, the spotters for instance being instructed in classes for aircraft recognition etc., and partly in Detachments comprising numbers 1 to 8 when we carried out imaginary engagements of 'targets' (as the aircraft was always known to us) with standard drill known as a 'manning drill' which always seemed to follow the same pattern, starting with 'target heard' and so to 'target seen' after which there was a crescendo of imaginary activities which always culminated in 'station attacked by low-flying aircraft – machine gun action' followed by the alarming order 'GAS' but eventually subsiding to 'target inaudible' and 'dowse'.

During the couverture we would be subject to Army discipline and apparently this made it necessary that the Army Act should be read to us. This was done on a parade outside the barracks one evening.

Captain Ingram did the actual reading and although he started in daylight, it went on so long, with section after section being read out, each one ending with the appropriate penalty which in nearly every case seemed to be death, that after a time the daylight failed and a sergeant had to stand by him with an electric torch.

There must have been four hundred men on parade. All of them had made sacrifices to join the Territorial Army and some of them would lose their lives in the impending war. These men stood there, motionless in the darkness while the voice droned on and on, threatening them with the death penalty. This made a very encouraging impression on me. While such things can happen, I said to myself, England will never lose a war.

2

THE FIRST DAYS

Most of those old enough to remember the declaration of war on Sunday, 3 September 1939 heard Neville Chamberlain's broadcast on BBC radio at 11 o'clock that morning. The crisis was precipitated when, on Friday, 1 September, Germany invaded Poland. At a tense and angry sitting of the House of Commons on the Saturday evening, many MPs had argued against further appeasement. As his broadcast made clear, Chamberlain himself hoped fervently that war could be averted, as it had been a year before:

> I am speaking to you from the Cabinet Room at 10 Downing Street.
>
> This morning the British Ambassador in Berlin handed the German Government a final note stating that, unless we heard from them by 11 o'clock that they were prepared at once to withdraw their troops from Poland, a state of war would exist between us. I have to tell you

Barrage balloons were dangerous and unwieldy, being on average 8.9m long and 7.6m in diameter. They were filled partially with hydrogen, partially with air, and were winched up usually from lorries and held in place by cables. Barrage balloons were essential defences against air attack as they forced all aircraft to fly higher around key areas such as industries, ports, towns and cities. This made bombers less accurate and helped anti-aircraft guns to aim more accurately.

now that no such undertaking has been received, and that consequently this country is at war with Germany.

You can imagine what a bitter blow it is to me that all my long struggle to win peace has failed. Yet I cannot believe that there is anything more or anything different that I could have done and that would have been more successful.

Up to the very last it would have been quite possible to have arranged a peaceful and honourable settlement between Germany and Poland, but Hitler would not have it. He had evidently made up his mind to attack Poland, whatever happened, and although he now says he put forward reasonable proposals which were rejected by the Poles, that is not a true statement.

The proposals were never shown to the Poles, nor to us, and though they were announced in a German broadcast on Thursday night, Hitler did not wait to hear comments on them but ordered his troops to cross the Polish frontier the next morning.

His action shows convincingly that there is no chance of expecting that this man will ever give up his practice of using force to gain his will. He can only be stopped by force. We and France are today, in fulfilment of our obligations, going to the aid of Poland, who is so bravely resisting this wicked and unprovoked attack upon her people. We have a clear conscience – we have done all that any country could do to establish peace.

The situation in which no word given by Germany's ruler could be trusted, and no people or country could feel itself safe, has become intolerable. And now that we have resolved to finish it I know that you will play your part with calmness and courage.

At such a moment as this the assurances of support which we have received from the Empire are a source of profound encouragement to us.

When I have finished speaking, certain detailed announcements will be made on behalf of the government. Give these your closest attention. The government have made plans under which it will be possible to carry on work of the nation in the days of stress and strain that may be ahead ...

Now may God bless you all. May He defend the right. For it is evil things that we shall be fighting against – brute force, bad faith, injustice, oppression and persecution – and against them I am certain that right will prevail.

For R.H. Lloyd-Jones, the outbreak of war seemed inevitable from the moment he heard of Germany's invasion of Poland:

On the morning of Friday, 1st September, we were taken in as usual to Section HQ at Wilden for concentration. During the morning's training on searchlight duties I noticed at one point that all the sound locators, instead of being pointed up in the air as they should have been, were in a horizontal position and directed towards one of the huts on the site. There was a news bulletin being read on the radio, and our listeners were receiving, in this unauthorized way, the first news that Germany had invaded Poland, meaning in effect that war was now inevitable.

As we left Wilden, to be driven back to our sites, cheerful shouts were exchanged between the occupants of the lorries, mostly to the effect that we would all see each other in Poland. One such shouted greeting has for some reason stuck in my memory; it was 'See you in Upper Silesia'. I don't think anyone nowadays would know or care where Upper Silesia was or is, but at that time it was a locality which was very much in the news.

On Sunday morning, 3rd September, arrangements had been made for a civilian hairdresser to visit the sites. Sitting on a spotter's chair in the middle of the field while having my hair cut I heard a radio set which someone had turned on, from which could be heard the very pleasant voice of Neville Chamberlain giving the not very pleasant news that we were now at war with Germany.

Parents and children reacted quite differently, as Leslie Gardiner – aged 12 in 1939 – remembered:

Those words had hardly left Mr Chamberlain's lips when the sirens sounded and we expected German planes to appear immediately. My father ushered my mother, my brother, me, and the dog down the garden to the Anderson shelter at the bottom of the garden.

As we hurried down the garden I looked over the fence to see our neighbour shepherding her two small children and carrying her small baby towards their shelter. What my brother and I found amusing was the fact that the two small children and their mother were wearing their gas masks and the baby was enveloped in a baby gas mask (a sort of large rubber envelope with a pump which had to be continuously pumped in order to keep the baby supplied with filtered air). Not so amusing for the harassed mother, but funny enough for a twelve and a twenty-one year old.

After a short time without any sign of the Luftwaffe, my brother decided to shovel some more earth on to the shelter which had been left, after its installation, with the light covering of soil which the workmen had given it. I offered to help big brother and we set to with a couple of garden spades. Apparently, inside the shelter, the sound of the stones rolling down the sides of the shelter sounded like gunfire and our mother urged us to re-enter the shelter at once. We did not do so, but redoubled our efforts with the spades so as to create the impression of a huge barrage. Our father then emerged from the shelter and upon discovering that we were teasing our mother threatened us with dire consequences if we did not desist. At that moment the all clear sounded and we had survived our first few hours of war.

In his autobiography, *Nine Lives*, Alan Deere, a New Zealand fighter pilot, recalled how the Royal Air Force (RAF) learned an important lesson that day:

On the first Sunday of the war, a lone aircraft return-ing from patrol was plotted as hostile and a squadron scrambled to investigate. This squadron became split and sections from it were in turn plotted as hostile, and more aircraft sent to investigate until eventually the opera-tions room tables, on which were plotted the raids, were cluttered with suspect plots. For about an hour, chaos reigned, and in this time nearly all the squadrons based to the east of London had been scrambled. I had trouble starting my aircraft and was late getting off and in the hour I was airborne spent the whole time trying to join up with my squadron which was receiving so many vectors [course instructions] that it was impossible to follow them. When I did eventually join up, the squadron was near Chatham where the anti-aircraft guns heralded our presence by some lusty salvoes, at which we hastily altered course despite the controller still insisting that we investigate the area. Not all the incidents … were amusing. 74 Squadron, led by 'Sailor' Malan, had also been sent off and their rear section of three encountered a pair of Hurricanes from nearby North Weald … in mistake for the enemy and in the excitement of this glorious muddle, they attacked and shot [them both] down, killing one of the pilots.

This truly amazing shambles – known to those pilots as the 'Battle of Barking Creek' – was just what was needed to iron out many snags in our control and reporting system and to convince those who were responsible that a great deal of controllers, plotters and radar operators, all of whom had been hastily drafted in on their first emergency call-up, was still required.

Betty Bullard, aged 21, volunteered for the ATS (Auxiliary Territorial Service), and was working on that first day in a recruitment office in Norwich. She recorded the day war broke out in her diary:

Sunday 3rd September 1939
A terrible day. Great depressions but a firm belief to the last that it couldn't really happen. Sat waiting by the wireless. At last a fine speech by Mr Chamberlain announcing 'a state of war between this country and Germany'. Series

of announcements. Black-out at night, cinemas closed, carry your gas mask, keep off roads at night etc etc.

It had come – decided to go to the sea with Geoffrey, Else and Margaret. Just arrived when message arrived for me to report at office at once. Went off in great excitement – all for nothing.

Monday 4th September 1939

Air raid warning 3 am, returned to hall feeling a little nervous but went to sleep on the floor. I still can't think of Germany as enemy and feel very sorry for wretched young pilots.

'Raiders past' and went to bed. Office moved to Agricultural Hall. Major Tully in uniform – much more military. Spent day getting … ready. Norwich much as usual. Digging up cattlemarket and everyone carries gasmask.

Friday 22nd September 1939

Went up to tea with Charlotte who is polishing up her German in case we lose the war!

I object to …

1) not being able to read in bed without having to grope about afterwards and open windows

2) being stared at in the street when walking about in uniform

3) getting no exercise (my own fault)

4) the noise the air raid warning makes. (A suggestion in the paper that they should play 'Who's afraid of the big bad wolf?' instead.)

Mollie Wilson, a teenager at this point living with her parents in Tyrone, Northern Ireland, wrote in her diary:

2nd September 1939

Mother and Daddy are so pessimistic we'll let Poland down, that they've given me the jitters. I feel just awful! Our house is in a good state of blackout. Worked all day painting blinds.

3rd September

When Chamberlain made his declaration of war, there was violent thunder and lightning, and rain shuttered down. I had always trusted rain too. No hostilities have begun but probably will have by tomorrow morning. All cinema shows and amusement have been prohibited as people are not to crowd together.

On the same day, in the log book for Warden's Post H85 at Paddington, London, the ARP warden on duty recorded: 'No first aid equipment, no formalin, no handbells' (bells were to be used to signal 'all clear' to civilians when a gas attack had been dealt with).

One year before, Conservative MP Duff Cooper had resigned from the Cabinet, where he had been First Lord of the Admiralty, over Chamberlain's appeasement of Hitler in Munich. On the day war was declared, Cooper was at a meeting of the small parliamentary group of people who supported Winston Churchill. Cooper wrote:

There at eleven o'clock we listened to the prime minister's broadcast statement that we were already at war with Germany. I recorded in my diary that 'we all thought he did it very well.' Our meeting broke up soon after he had finished as the house was meeting at noon. As we left the house we heard strange sounds and said, laughing, that it

sounded like an air-raid warning, which indeed it proved
to be. We walked on towards the House of Commons –
Anthony, Derek Gullston and I. Derek said, 'We're walking
pretty fast, aren't we?' which we were. When we arrived
there we were directed to a room opposite the downstairs smoking-room, which was full of an odd mixture of
people – servants, typists and the Speaker. We didn't stay
there long but wandered out on the terrace, where we
watched the balloons go up, which they did with great
speed. It was a beautiful morning. The house met at twelve
as arranged and the all clear signal went during prayers. I
did not think the prime minister so good as he had been
on the radio, nor did I think any of the speeches reached a
very high level. Greenwood's was about the best.

I took Terence O'Connor out to luncheon at Buck's.
We both envied the people we saw there in uniform.
They at least have something to do – and plenty to do. I
have nothing.

Despite the warning that sounded in the South-East almost
as soon as the declaration of war had been broadcast, the mass
raids people feared would arrive immediately did not come.
Over the next year, while German U-boats and the Luftwaffe
attacked British merchant ships carrying food and other
vital supplies into Britain, very little happened on the home
front. People soon became bored by the air raid precautions
that punctuated daily life. ARP wardens who enforced the
blackout and exhorted people to carry their gas masks were a
source of considerable irritation and comment.

A letter published in *The Times* from H. De Pree of
Beckley, on 21 September 1939, reflected a popular view-
point. He argued that the ARP was:

an appalling waste of public money … excessive fear of gas bombardment in country districts [meant that] thousands of pounds have been wasted on useless equipment.

Much of the expensive and overstaffed organisation would, he said, never be used:

Payment of £2 or £3 a week to men to stand about doing nothing is causing notable resentment among genuine workers in the country whose ordinary wages are under £2. Incidentally, the same feeling is aroused with regard to the excessive wages which are being paid by contractors to workmen on huts, &c., under construction for the government in many places.

He added that anti-aircraft fire would be the best warning for those living in country districts and, 'based on this premise the whole of our ARP organization outside really important areas should be drastically cut down, especially as regards paid personnel'.

The ARP wardens' log for Post 85 in Maida Vale, London, puts it more succinctly:

23rd September 1939
21.40hrs: Watch lights at 265 Lauderdale Avenue. Man most insulting.

24th September 1939
Lauderdale Mansions, Lauderdale Avenue, light at back. Man showed most uncompromising attitude. Above reported to police … If light shows again, please ask for police to no. 64, and take him round to show him light.

Phillip Chignell recalled the horror of air raids that he and his wife had experienced during the First World War in Hessle, a town on the edge of Kingston upon Hull. He wrote to his sister about the impact of the declaration of war:

Tuesday 5th September 1939
My dear Ruth ...

I am just going to tell you how it has affected us all at Hessle. My first remark is that it has broken up our little family circle. All our four children have lived at home ever since they were born. You may not approve of this system but that is not the point. There are six of us, as you know, and we have all lived happily together until this time when Herr Hitler seems to have set Europe on fire with his terrible ambition. Of course we knew that something in the way of another war was brewing. It has not come upon us as a terrible surprise. The business seemed to have a definite beginning when Trigo came home from school on Wednesday with definite instructions about the school evacuation that had been arranged some time ago ... On Thursday she went off to school with everything as arranged, temporary luggage, sufficient food to last. She came home at dinner time although we had not expected her and she then and there definitely refused to be evacuated, she just declined to go. We did not attempt any argument but we insisted that she return to the Boulevard school and tell them that she would not be evacuated. She went back and returned home for tea.

About 6.45 I went off to the bowling club and I left John having his tea in the usual manner. When I returned home at 8.00 to listen to the Promenade concert, John

Established fire brigades needed to increase their size many times over to meet the demands of air raids in wartime. The shortfall was made up by the creation of the Auxiliary Fire Service and the Women's Auxiliary Fire Service (the AFS and the WAFS). Here in 1939 is WAFS driver Cathcart in London.

had gone. A dispatch rider had called for him and he had packed up and gone off at once. He left a form filled up to be posted to Smith and Nephew to say why he should be away from his work the next morning. We have not seen John since that day, but we now know that he is near Spurn Head with a gun battery …

Of course you know that Katie and I lived in Hull all through the trying time, 1914–1918, when there were many air raids by Zeppelins. It is no new thing for me to hear gunfire or bombing in actual warfare and it is no new thing for me to experience the sickening sensation that comes to most of us when we know we are in the danger zone of aerial attack. I remember how father used to ridicule us for feeling like this and I sometimes wished that he had had at least one experience of an air raid. Nobody knows what it is like until they have had the experience. So Katie and I are not novices in this respect. We both feel we had our fair share 25 years ago and now we may have to bear the worry and trouble of it all over again.

At tea-time (on Friday 1st September) a dispatch rider called, this time it was for Henry. He packed up and was off in half an hour. Katie packed food for him and he went saying goodbye to us. We did not know when we should see him again or where he was going … The vicar telephoned to me – on no account was I to have a light in the church or the vestry after 8 pm. (re choir practice) …

Harry returned home late last night – the authorities did not know how to sleep the 1,300 young men who had answered the call and most were sent home.

Ann Maxtone Graham returned by ship – without her sons – in these early, nervous days. Her London neighbours,

Jane and Bob Badham, and their son Michael (aged 13 when war was declared), met her at Southampton. At the start of the war Jane and Michael had left London for the Berkshire village of Wargrave:

Jane said that she was wakened one night by Anna creeping into the room and whispering 'Jane, Jane, the sirens have gone.' They switched on the light, trying not to waken Michael. He, however, heard and said, 'what is it, a warning? Oh.' And he proceeded to read quite calmly while the other two quaked inwardly. Jane, in her excitement, filed her nails almost to the quick. At last she could not bear it any longer and went to turn up a tiny corner of the blackout curtain so that she could peer out and see what, if anything, was happening. To her complete surprise, it was broad daylight, and the gardener was bicycling up the drive with his gas mask on.

After two or three days, as things were quiet and there had been no raids, Bob had let them come back to London. There they had been ever since, living, as far as I could see, a perfectly normal life. And that's what I was going to do, go [home] to no 45 as usual. Somehow it made everything seem so much easier to bear, to be going home, although I confess with shame, a little flat. It was like making your mind to jump off a high place and coming down about six inches. I had visions of myself dodging bombs and being homeless. Well, thank goodness, I had a home and, so far, no bombs.

When we got to London and started towards South Kensington, I nearly fell out of the taxi looking up at the lovely silver barrage balloons that floated high over the city. I had seen a few, but never so many as there were now. Hundreds of them, like little silver fish swimming in the evening sky. There were sandbags – sandbags everywhere, stacked against windows, built into tidy walls to protect doorways, and around police call boxes. In those days they were fresh and new, but as winter went on they rotted and burst, and at last a great many of them were taken away.

Home at last, and I felt as if the war was a dream. Number 45 Tregunter Road looked natural and just as it had always done when I'd come home to it before. At least it did until I opened the front door and found a funereal gloom. The blackout. I had forgotten it. Our hall and stairway had such odd windows that they couldn't be curtained. And the only thing to do was to cover them up with thick black cloth, firmly thumbtacked around the edges. We used to untack a small corner in the morning and pin it back, and then down it went again as soon as it grew dark. Oh, the thumbtack holes in my nice white paint! I felt I couldn't bear it at first, but after a few days one hole more or less didn't seem to matter. Once coming down the dark stairs I heard myself mutter, 'bloody old mole, that's what I am!'

… All this time my family in America kept writing and condoling with me on the horrible times I was living through. It was then that Judy wrote, 'I can't make any picture of how you live. Do you slink from cellar to cellar?' No matter what I wrote to them, they still persisted in thinking of me as a frightened, panic-stricken female, I'm afraid my letters to them were a little profane at this time, partly because I felt like a humbug having all this undeserved pity and worry poured out on me.

... Life was more or less normal. It was a queer time, knowing that there was a war but nothing dire seemed to be happening in England. I missed Pat and the boys more than I could say, and it was hard being alone.

But all those things I had got used to and I had Jane and Bob right around the corner. The nights I didn't go to them, they came to me. I made myself laugh, starting out to spend a pleasant evening, gas mask over my shoulder, knitting under my arm, flashlight in one hand and a cane in the other. I used to walk with this like a blind man to save the battery in my flashlight, as they were hard to come by at the moment.

... it was curious how the days flew. I suppose when you are busy they do fly. It seemed to me about five minutes from one blackout to another. It was odd how we got used to that, too, and couldn't quite remember what it was like to have lived in the days before the war when you didn't have to turn out the hall light before you opened the front door. How horrified and indignant we were if we saw a chink of light from a neighbour's house. The wardens and police were wonderful and spotted them almost at once. Sometimes they weren't very polite about it and roared, 'Put out that light!'

I couldn't blame them, for people were tiresome about it and acted as if they had been mortally insulted. Instead of being sorry and apologetic, they were rude and unpleasant when told there was a light showing. After all, they would have been the first to squeal if a bomb had come crashing down on their heads. But the warden said you couldn't make them realise it.

I was told that the British drove trucks or tanks over the moors to make it look like roads. Even flashed

occasional light so that the Germans might think there
were towns there. I believe they did and wasted a lot of
bombs on empty spaces that might well have come down
on houses and people.

R.H. Lloyd-Jones was posted as permanent staff instructor to 231 Searchlight Training Regiment soon after
the war started. He travelled to camp at Blandford
near Bournemouth:

> As we worked on the arrangements for receiving our first
> intake, as it was called, it was obvious that we were in for
> a busy time. There were well over a thousand men, due to
> arrive, all on the same day, all needing to be documented
> and fed and issued with their kit and allotted to living huts.
> We were in the Gym as the men came off the lor-
> ries that brought them from the station. There was much
> paperwork involved and many of the Intake seemed to
> be under strain. They had to be asked details of their
> families; some could not remember their children's
> names, one or two could not even remember their own
> names. I saw one recruit weeping and being patted on
> the shoulder by Capt. St Barbe in an attempt to cheer
> him up. Thank goodness we never had this emotional
> atmosphere again with any other Intake. As the war con-
> tinued, it seemed men became less sensitive to the shock
> of being called up.

J.L. Stevens was 13 in 1939. She saw the battles fought over
the English Channel and the North Sea, and the RAF's
efforts to counter the naval mines laid by the Luftwaffe:

I had had rheumatic fever when I was 11 years old and had mitral stenosis so I no longer attended school. In April 1940, I was sent to a convalescent home situated on the cliffs at Broadstairs, Kent. We were allowed to write home once a week.

I had been very interested in the planes which swooped low over the sea as they had large rings fitted and I had seen nothing like this. I was very keen on drawing so in one of my letters to my parents I drew a picture of such a plane. I did not know that all our letters were censored by the matron – really to erase our adverse comments regarding the home – but my drawing was blacked out. Later, of course, I found that the rings [were to set off] magnetic mines.

Adults and children alike were curious as much as they were fearful of enemy planes, so much so that people were told specifically to take cover rather than go into the street to watch the raid – common practice during Zeppelin raids of the First World War.

The first civilian death from enemy aerial action on British soil in the Second World War was James Isbister, who died on the doorstep of his Orkney island home on 16 March 1940 when a Junkers Ju 88 returning from a raid on the naval base at Scapa Flow jettisoned its remaining bombs. The raid and its aftermath were reported in the *Daily Record* for 20 March 1940:

The only inhabitant today of the half-wrecked hamlet of the Bridge of Waithe, in the West mainland of the Orkney islands is Mrs Farquhar, a widow of almost 70 years of age. On Saturday evening she escaped death in the German air raid. Her son, William Farquhar, was wounded while standing with his mother in their little confectionery shop-cum-boot-repairing establishment. On Sunday Mrs. Farquhar's little shop was conducted by a friend, Mrs. John Scott, of Nether Onston, Stenness. Yesterday and to-day, in a shop and house darkened by wood-shuttered windows, Mrs. Farquhar mopped up after the bombing. Every window in the house and in the little hamlet is blown out or in. Between sweeping out debris, Mrs. Farquhar is philosophically serving customers, most of them workmen, with chocolate biscuits, lemonade, cigarettes, etc. Next door is the shuttered and silent house of tragedy, the home of James Isbister, who was killed outright when hit on the head as one of a batch of bombs burst opposite the buildings. Over the week-end the young widow, formerly Miss Lily Tait, of Kirkwall, sister of the Rev. Thomas G. Tait, minister of Rendall Parish, Orkney Islands, was cared for at Upper Onston, the home of relatives, near the scene of the bombing. Today it is hoped to convey her to the Kirkwall home of her widowed mother. Mrs Isbister escaped injury by a miracle. Her husband was struck down only moments after she had gone in from her door to look at her sleeping child, a boy born last December. She is prostrate with grief.

Similarly, the first deaths from enemy aerial action in England were not from a planned attack on civilians. A Heinkel bomber crashed in May 1940 while laying mines off the coast of Clacton-on-Sea in Essex. Mr and Mrs W. Gill of Victoria Road, Clacton-on-Sea, were killed, along with the four-man crew of the plane. All that remained of the

Gills' house was a mound of bricks; their son William was one of the thirty-four who were seriously injured among a total of 156 people that were wounded.

The War Illustrated was published during the First World War and, as a weekly, in the Second World War and afterwards until early 1947. Its report of the Clacton crash, published on 17 May 1940, drew entirely on eye-witness accounts:

Mrs E.F. Thomas saw the plane crash:

The plane was on fire. Several Very lights [signal flares] were thrown out of it and the pilot was apparently trying to find some place to land. Fifty yards up Victoria Road the plane hit the road, bounced through the side of a house and then went clean through two other houses, smashing them to pieces. A few minutes later there was an explosion ...

Miss Joyce Redding, of Russell Road, said: 'One extraordinary thing was that, although every window was shattered and blackout materials were torn down, the electricity was not cut off and the district was a blaze of light. When half an hour afterwards an unknown plane flew overhead wardens hurried around shouting 'lights out, lights out'.

Kenneth Harper, aged 17, a friend of William Gill, added:

I saw the plane, which had been careering round the district for about half an hour, hit a house. One wing of it was left in the garden of that house, and it went over the Gills' house, knocking down a tree and coming to a standstill.

I ran up to within about thirty-five yards of it when I heard a terrific explosion. The next thing I knew was debris flying all about me, and I put my arms around my head and ran. I had a very narrow escape. Bricks were flying all around. Bill Gill apparently got his father into the garden and went back for his mother, but the house collapsed before he could get her out. I suppose he found his mother was trapped and then he ran to get other help. Then, while he was out, the house collapsed entirely. When he reached us young Gill was without his shoes and his shirt was just about blown off him.

Brig-Gen W.M. Fordham, deputy chief ARP warden of Clacton, who lives in the road in which the bomber crashed, said he and his neighbours rushed to the scene. 'There was no panic,' he said. 'The injured people were quickly attended to and taken to hospital. The ARP personnel showed that they have been well-trained. They were quick, and yet as cool and efficient as if they were on one of our usual exercises.'

Gen. Fordham added that the fire brigade and the AFS also did remarkably well. 'This terrible crash,' he said, 'has provided the biggest test to which any town's ARP service could expect to be put. I am proud of the way our fellows stood up to it.'

The *Irish Times* was more critical:

[The fact that the] plane was circling overhead for so long before it finally fell was responsible both for some extraordinarily fine work by the town's ARP personnel and for a large number of injuries which might have been avoided.

Many people were in the streets or looking out of windows when the crash came, and were cut by flying fragments of glass or pieces of bricks and tiles.

As a chief air raid warden said: 'One lesson to be learned from the explosion is that people who had taken cover were uninjured, and an air raid shelter within a few yards of the crater in which the wreckage of the bomber lay was completely undamaged.'

Some residents were inclined to criticise the authorities for not giving an air raid warning. 'I think,' said one of them, 'that most of the people who were injured were hurt because either they were looking out of their windows, having heard the plane overhead for so long, or were sleeping in upper rooms and had tiles fall in on them. Had they been in lower rooms or in a shelter the majority might not have been hurt at all.'

RAIDERS OVERHEAD AND CONTINUING PREPARATIONS

In the spring of 1940, German forces launched their Blitzkrieg ('lightning war') against western Europe. In Britain, Neville Chamberlain resigned as Prime Minister on 10 May 1940. The disastrous Allied campaign in Norway had failed to halt the German invasion of that country. He was replaced by Winston Churchill.

At the end of May, British and Allied troops were hastily rescued from the beaches of Dunkirk in France. By the end of June, most of western Europe had capitulated – only Britain fought on against Hitler. In these early stages, the Luftwaffe carried out scattered attacks and mine-laying sorties targeting towns with war industries, ports, shipping and the RAF Chain Home radar stations, where the newly developed device proved vital, giving Britain's anti-aircraft defences and the RAF fighters warning of the approaching bombers.

From 17 July to 12 August, there were more frequent daylight attacks, by more bombers, against shipping in the English Channel, ports along the south and east coasts and some coastal airfields.

Members of ARP in a report centre. Reports came in by telephone or from bicycle messengers detailing incidents; locations of ambulances, fire services, first-aid parties, and rescue and repair services; buildings damaged and where casualties might be found; where roads were blocked; and where water or gas mains were damaged. The chart on the wall displayed this essential information and services were organised from the centre. *Courtesy of* Kent Messenger

Night attacks targeted the West, the Midlands, the east coast, RAF facilities and the aircraft industry. Britain's anti-aircraft defences such as searchlights and anti-aircraft guns, as well as passive defence such as air raid wardens, ambulance and fire services, were still under strength in the summer of 1940. Attempts by fighter aircraft to attack the bombers at night had proved disastrous.

Henry Beckingham was too young to go overseas when war broke out. When his company went to France as part of the British Expeditionary Force, he moved to another unit of the Royal Engineers. His account shows how, even at this late stage, Britain was poorly prepared:

Early in May 1940 I was in the courtyard at Borwick Hall when the Sergeant Major came up to me and asked me if I would like to go on a course to Sheffield. He also hinted that if I went on the course it would give me the opportunity of being allowed a weekend leave to be with my family in Manchester.

The following morning Lance Corporal Acton, Sapper Andrews and myself left Borwick and arrived in Sheffield. Little did we know then that we were to form one of the first bomb disposal parties in England.

Our course did in fact only last one day, at the end of which we were given a drawing which showed how to deal with an unexploded bomb (UXB). It was assumed that any UXB would be found on the surface. The drawing showed how to build a sandbagged wall to which was added further sandbags. A small crawl-way was to be left in the wall to enable one to crawl in and place a charge on the bomb casing and thus detonate it in situ.

We were then issued with a requisitioned old Austin car and told to carry out a thorough reconnaissance of the city so that in the event of an air attack, we could go directly to any incident. Arrangements had also to be made to organise suitable store areas around the city where stocks of sandbags, corrugated sheeting, picks, and shovels could be kept.

We were attached to an RASC [Royal Army Service Corps] unit which was stationed at Endcliffe Hall, Sheffield, for pay and rations only. During the summer of 1940 we spent a pleasant time touring Sheffield and many afternoons playing table tennis in the YMCA [Young Men's Christian Association]; in short we languished in idle obscurity waiting for something to happen …

Our salvation came at the beginning of September when Lieut. Godsmark arrived in Sheffield with men of the 35th Bomb Disposal Section R.E. [Royal Engineers].

One consequence of the unexpected inactivity at the very start of the war was that many children who had been evacuated away from cities and other danger areas in the early days had returned home by the time raids started. J. Grenville Atherton, then a 15-year-old schoolboy, recalled his return to Stretford, Greater Manchester:

We returned to Stretford from Macclesfield on our first day back at school on Friday 19th April 1940. Mr Albert Dakin the headmaster happily welcomed us. To ensure our safety he explained that all ground floor corridors were being modified and strengthened to make adequately-sized air raid shelters for the whole school, and that furniture and equipment was ready for use. He gave us a half day holiday, we gave him a spontaneous cheer and he expected to see us at 9 am the following Monday when lessons commenced more or less as they were in 1939 before the interruption of evacuation.

During the weekend one of my father's friends on the council showed him a notice from the town hall personnel department inviting applications for the post of assistant air raid precautions officer at £400 per annum. It listed 16 ministers to whom the applicant would ultimately be responsible. My father thought it was a joke.

In his diary for 1940, he recorded the first air raid warning in Stretford:

Today 20th June full moon 12.02 am
Stretford had its first Wailing Winnie siren air alarm at 3.30 am. I put on my new sports jacket over my pyjamas and white gym pumps. My mother, father and sister just sat in the darkness and we opened the curtains. Our eyes became accustomed to the dark and the moonlight highlighted the polish on the furniture. We heard voices in the road; ARP wardens. We thought it was quiet. We were ready to dive under the heavy oak table if needs be (we had no shelter then) but it was not necessary. After half an hour Dad went back to bed. We sat and dozed until the 'raiders passed' siren sounded at 4.15 am.

Planes had dropped bombs on north eastern England and south Wales.

The next day we had another air raid warning from 1.10 am to 2.15 am but no raiders put in an appearance.

Some parts of the United Kingdom did not expect to see the enemy at first hand. Pembroke in Wales had a rude awakening as Bill Richards, chief reporter of the *West Wales Guardian*, who lived and worked in the town, recalled later:

July 10th, 1940, will live forever in Pembrokeshire's history for it was on that day that the county took the first shock of an enemy air attack. The air raid itself, carried out by a solitary plane, was a fairly minor affair compared with what was to come, but will probably be remembered, as at 10.12 am, without any warning, the town was rocked by a terrific explosion. There had been no siren and in those days an air raid without warning was unthinkable (how we were to learn!). All the many shops and offices workers looked at each other a trifle pale, and murmured 'Bombs.' Nothing happened. The sound of not even one could be heard. Perhaps it wasn't a bomb after all … Then, at 10.20, all speculation was ended by the sounding of the siren … It was an air raid all right. A few minutes later the raider came in again across the town. There it was for all to see, a big, black Junkers 88, flying from east to west, high and close to the heavy blanket of cloud. I had ventured, albeit with extreme caution, from the 'Guardian' Office as far as the Bird in Hand in Lewis Street, and from the pavement there watched the plane in company with the genial landlord, Alderman Joe Gibby … As we watched, two black specks appeared beneath the plane. 'Birds,' said I, with more hope than conviction. 'Birds be d--d,' exclaimed Ald. Gibby, a veteran of 1914–18. 'They're bombs, come on in.' The explosions did not seem quite so terrifying from a crouching position beside the bar! Two stiff whiskies a few moments later (out of hours) did much to restore the equilibrium of both of us! During the next few minutes there were further explosions, between which machine-gun fire was heard coming from the Barrack Hill where some soldiers were 'having a go' at the intruder. At the time many people feared the streets were being machine-gunned. In all the excitement the sounding of the town siren – about twenty minutes late – went almost unnoticed. Some ten minutes later the Junkers flew away down south to return to its base, where, according to a later German news bulletin, the pilot reported 'a heavy raid on Pembroke where large fires were started.' Actually, the damage caused by this raider, in what must have been one of the easiest assignments any bomber crew could ever have had, was infinitesimal. The first bomb which so shook the town fell in the harbour between Neyland and Pembroke Dock … Had it fallen in the town it would doubtless have wreaked tremendous havoc … but miraculously no one was hit. The only casualties were scores of fish which, killed or stunned by the explosion, came to the surface and were washed ashore – to provide many a tasty meal for the people living in the Llanion area.

The other bombs, four or five in number and of smaller calibre, fell in and around Llanreath. This pilot was evidently after the oil tanks and although it was not generally known at the time, one bomb found its mark. But luck was with Pembroke Dock that day and the tank did not blow up. The bomb must have been a dud! Evidence of the raider's marksmanship was provided by a neat hole in the top of one of the tanks. Delayed action bombs being little heard of in those days, many people climbed a ladder to examine the cavity – and, months later, shivered at the very thought of it! This air raid, the first of many, was the sole topic of conversation in

Pembroke Dock that day and for several days afterwards. To the rest of the county it was a matter of great interest but to the Borough of Pembroke it was one of vital concern. Pembroke Dock became really A.R.P. conscious overnight and braced itself to meet a grim period ahead. The townspeople were taken aback by the air raid itself but there was far greater concern at the almost complete defencelessness of the area and the fact that the siren was so late giving warning. We were soon to learn by grim experience that anti-aircraft defences in Pembrokeshire were almost non-existent and that the system of warning was to take many months to become efficient. In fact, during those early days, bombs-before-siren became the rule. By the time the siren became of any use the enemy was beginning to switch his attentions elsewhere.

The prospect of a German invasion put the quiet east coast town of Southwold in Suffolk on the front line. As in other coastal areas, its beach was covered with barbed wire and hundreds of mines were laid along the shoreline. A hole was made in its pier to prevent it being used to disembark invading German troops; two 6in guns were installed in the front garden of a seafront villa near Gun Hill to defend the town against naval attacks. The invasion never came but Southwold was frequently attacked by low-flying aircraft that swept in from the North Sea below radar cover.

Tom King began work in July 1940 as an ARP telephonist in Southwold police station. In 1940, Tom was aged 35, and married with two young daughters, Rita and Liz. He was exempt from military service because he had had a leg amputated. His wartime diary reflects the long periods of quiet punctuated by bursts of frenetic activity, as raiders hit coastal towns and airfields:

July 14 1940
Weather fine, began duties at 10 pm till 8 am for one week. Had a red warning at 10 pm, all clear eight minutes later, 2nd warning at 3.15 am lasting for four minutes, at 5 am a yellow warning. PC Riches on duty.

Tuesday July 16th
Weather heavy rain all night.
Very quiet, no warnings, played cards with PC Guilliatt to pass the time away. PC Riches on duty from midnight.

Monday July 22nd
... new warning colours came through today. Purple is for dousing light, this washes out green.
Lights for warning are now yellow, first warning; red for action; purple as above; white for all clear.

Thursday July 25th
Weather fine early morning, cloudy later in the day.
Five yellows during the night. Very quiet in the morning and afternoon only one yellow, time drags – shall have to find a hobby.

31st July
Took Rita round the harbour and the marshes in the morning. She is a good girl and enjoyed the walk. Was pretty busy up to midnight when I came on duty. Played cards with the Inspector, Jarvis and Miss Allen. Taking the whole night it was the most active we had had. I gave out

eighteen calls before going home for breakfast. At 1.00 we had a red through, I was in charge and switched on the siren for the first time, we also had two purples. At 2.15 pm three salvos of bombs were dropped about two miles off the town into the sea. Bombs were also dropped between Dunwich and Wickham Market.

8th August

One red during the night and another at 6 am lasting until 6.50. On duty at 08.00 I heard an explosion at 08.28 am, report said that a bullock had strayed on to the beach and stepped on a mine. It blew the bull to pieces.

That summer, Mollie Wilson left her home in Tyrone and joined the WAAF. She was stationed at West Drayton in Middlesex – her diary was confiscated by customs as she entered Britain. She wrote to her parents about her first experience of a raid:

WAAF training depot West Drayton

12th August 1940

Dearest Mother and Daddy

I was coming to supper (yesterday) when I heard the wailing siren, followed by our own whistles (we pay no attention to outside warnings) and boy! Did I run or did I run! I wasn't scared, but in our own room we had been told to arrange a fire picket, and we forgot. So I rushed up the stairs and carried down a pail of sand, a fire extinguisher and a bucket of water to put outside the block. Some other girls carried down the other three buckets. Then I grabbed my mac, my gas clothing and mask, and ran. I slipped on the stairs and fell six steps but only

bruised myself a bit. We all got into our trenches all right
and sat for about ten minutes till the all clear came. The
Germans must have been a long way off for we didn't see
anything of them at all. It was jolly nice of Hitler to let
us have the warning in the daytime and we were still in
time for our concert ...

... when I got as far as this we had another warning,
12.30. We stayed in the trenches until 1.20 but nothing
happened again. I was a bit cross, 'cause I was terribly
hungry but for dessert we had banana and ice-cream so
it was worth it.

From 13 August to 6 September, the Luftwaffe carried
out large-scale attacks on the airfields of RAF Fighter
Command in south-east England. This was seen – and presented – as the prelude to the Nazi invasion of Britain. Any
plan to invade Britain depended on defeating the Royal
Navy. This could only be done by first taking command
of the air, so the Luftwaffe aimed to destroy the airfields
of RAF Fighter Command. Alan Deere was now at RAF
Manston, a few miles inland from Ramsgate, the eastern-
most part of Kent:

For some time now, the Germans had been waiting for
a day in which the weather would prove favourable
enough to land a concentrated effort against our northern and southern fighter bases. It would thus be possible
for them to determine to what extent our defences in the
north had been stripped to supplement the hard-pressed
squadrons in the south. August 15th was the chosen
day ... The first wave, consisting of about sixty Ju 87s
[Stuka dive-bombers] escorted by an equal number of

109s [Messerschmitt fighters] and with Lympne as their target, was met by 54 Squadron as it crossed the coast between Dover and Dungeness. Against such odds, it was impossible to prevent the bombers reaching their target. Nevertheless we did manage to get among the Junkers 87s and to harass them throughout their attack, despite the presence of the 109s. It was an impressive sight … A mere handful of Spitfires altered the picture very little as, virtually lost in a maze of 109s, they strove to interfere …

The first raid of the day had crossed the coast near Dover at 11.20 am and the last enemy aircraft departed our shores at approximately 7.25 pm, when a heavily mauled force of Me [Messerschmitt] 110s, which had attacked Croydon airfield – an uncomfortable reminder to Londoners that the air battle was moving on to them – retreated to their lair in occupied territory.

In that short period of time I had been airborne on six occasions. Some idea of the intensity of operations can be gauged from the fact that a normal sortie averaged 40 minutes, and that on four occasions re-arming and refuelling was necessary.

So 15th August closed. The enemy had launched six major assaults – and many minor ones also in the south-east against airfields as far as Acklington in Northumberland to Middle Wallop in Hampshire. In all two thousand enemy aircraft had been hurled against our shores in successive waves only to be met by a deter-mined defence which, although penetrated on occasions, never failed to close the gaps …

Nightfall brought blessed relief to the weary pilots of the 11th Group squadrons who had once again borne the brunt of the attack. To me the reverse was true; I was shot

down on the last sortie of the day and spent five ago-
nizing hours in the back of an RAF ambulance which
bounced and bumped its way through the blacked-out
highways and by-ways of Kent in search of Kenley airfield, only to finish up at the Queen Victoria Hospital,
East Grinstead.

Mary Baker was one of many children evacuated to
Tonbridge in Kent:

The Battle of Britain began while I was there. The sight
of planes being shot down and parachutes falling is as
vivid today as it was then. One day there was a terrified
young German airman under guard in the town. I admit
I felt quite sorry for him as he looked so scared.

London's main civilian airport at Croydon became an RAF
fighter station in the Second World War. On that Thursday,
15 August, German planes overshot the airfield – their
intended target – and most of their bombs fell on a local
aircraft factory, a perfume factory and a nearby housing
estate. The sirens sounded seventeen minutes after the first
bombs fell. Sixty-two people were killed, thirty-seven seriously injured and 137 less seriously injured. Cecil Beaton,
well known in the 1930s as a fashion and society photographer, was appointed an official war photographer and
was an air raid warden at the outbreak of war. In his diary
he recorded his visit to view the aftermath:

Went to Croydon to see real air raid damage. It is pathetic!
The sirens didn't go off and 300 women and girls [this is
an overestimate] were killed in factories there. The relics

are poignant: a picture of the King and royal family among the cardboard containers that lie by the thousand among the white cocaine-like debris! A residential quarter also suffered, and one dwelling – luckily deserted – was completely demolished, its art nouveau decorations scattered far and wide. If you go there you'll find an unexploded bomb maybe a dud – maybe a delayed action. Better keep this side of the fence: Along one road, where a stick of bombs dropped, they've made a guy of Hitler, railed off a section and collected scrap iron, twelve and a half tons of it! In Germany everything is done by order. Here much is left to personal spontaneous effort. The funeral processions pass down the highway; everyone is calm and quiet. But one street beyond, life goes on as if nothing had happened, as if nothing could happen from one particular day to another – unless of course our number is called and, if it is, we are not likely to know it, luckily.

Jim Purdey lived in the town and in 1940 his mother was in ARP. Jim remembered:

Early in 1940 brick-built ARP wardens posts were provided. These were about twenty-five feet by ten feet, with a flat reinforced roof and a door in the end elevation which was protected by a blast wall. There were no windows. Each post could hold about twelve people, and that was about the average number of wardens to each post.

Early in the war the name ARP was changed to Civil Defence and the Chief Warden for Croydon was a man named Captain Smith. Croydon was divided into districts and South Norwood became 'H' district, under the

Nanci Nicholls, leader of a Mobile Medical unit, in her uniform; the (red) braid around the collar of her civil defence raincoat shows she is a nurse; the badge on her helmet is that of St Pancras in London.

control of a District Warden whose name was Mr Luther. There were about six sectors in South Norwood, I can only remember H33 near to Goat House bridge, H39 in Regina Road, H45 in Manor Road, H50 headquarters in Harrington Road, and another one in Dingwall Road. Each post was under the control of a post Warden who had his three full timers and as many part timers as he could get. Thinking back on it today, I cannot remember any lady being in a senior position, although there were possibly more lady wardens than men. It was simply a sign of the times.

In late 1940 I became a warden myself. We were taught simple first aid, how to recognise poison gas, deal with incendiary bombs and report incidents on our sector. We learned that each poison gas has its own distinctive smell and exposed itself to anti-gas paint. The tops of pillar boxes and squares of wood fixed at a sloping angle were painted with anti-gas paint, so that droplets of liquid gas changed colour as they dribbled downwards. If we saw this we then had to raise the alarm by using wooden rattles, similar to rattles used at football matches. Thankfully this drill was never carried out.

Incendiary bombs were another hazard. They were about 18 inches long and 3 inches in diameter, they burst on impact and showered the area with magnesium fire. They were dealt with by using a stirrup pump, or a bucket of sand or soil. One aircraft could carry a large load of incendiaries and cause fires over a wide area. In Croydon all roof attics were inspected and cleared of all combustible materials. The situation regarding incendiaries became so serious that people had to take turns at firewatching at their place of employment. This meant they had to stay at their workplace all night ready to tackle any incendiaries. A stirrup pump was a hand-operated pump that delivered a jet or spray of water. It took three persons to operate: one to pump; one to direct the jet or spray, and one to replenish the water in the bucket. If the bomb was in an open area a bucket of soil on it usually did the trick.

Bombs that failed to explode were another hazard. They could be defective or they could be one with a delayed fuse. These could explode unexpectedly up to three or four days later, and all had to be investigated by the bomb disposal people, by digging them out and taking them away and exploding them safely. This was a very dangerous occupation.

When a bomb exploded it caused utter devastation at the point of impact, and damage occurred over a wide area. At the edge of the radius of damage there usually were two sorts of damage. The first you noticed was that most of the windows were missing, usually blown inwards. One trick that everyone did was to criss-cross their windows with strips of sticky brown tape. This allowed the entire pane of glass to come in, in one piece. It prevented the glass from shattering, and prevented many injuries from shards of sharp glass flying everywhere. The window opening was then sealed with squares of what today we call plastic sheeting, which was fixed with battens. Although you could not see through this material, it did let the light in and kept the weather out.

Another noticeable damage was that the blast caused roof tiles to shuffle up the roof about six inches, thus causing the roof to become unwatertight. Slate roofs were not so bad, but with tiles, they had to be pulled down back into position one at a time, with the use of a flat trowel, a very time-consuming task.

Even a small bomb caused damage to water, electricity, gas and sewerage services, some of which took a long time to become noticeable.

On the Suffolk coast, Tom King went into action when the town of Southwold was bombed for the first time on 20 August:

Weather – Dull cool day.

Had three reds during the night and early morning. Had one red through in the morning, three German bombers dropped bombs at Pakenham and Oulton, one German plane was brought down for certain. Red through again at 13.45, lasting for 10 minutes.

We had our first bombing of the town, first raid started at 15.50. Two bombs landed in the back gardens of council houses in Hotson road, no particular damage to property, only windows broken. The second raid started at 18.05, plane came in from the sea and started dropping bombs in the sea, one landed on the cliff, one in the back of the vicarage and Glan-y-don by Mr Fisher's, and one between Field Style road and Hotson road, finishing in the hard courts. All told we had nineteen HE bombs dropped and four incendiary bombs, these fell near the pier, one fell in the station yard, and one on the marshes.

Damage done – vicarage roof and Glan-y-don red roof premises severely damaged. Mr Bolderstone's house received a direct hit, Mr and Mrs Bolderstone injured also Mrs Sage who was in the house at the time of the occurrence. Main services in action, demolition and road repair gang. The ambulance took the three casualties to hospital. Incendiary bombs fell in the surrounding district.

Vera Brittain, the author, feminist and pacifist, was a fire warden based in Kensington at the start of the war. A leading member of the Peace Pledge Union, she campaigned against saturation bombing. Her name was on the Sonderfahndungsliste G.B. (Special Search List GB), the Nazis' 'black book' of names of people who were to be rounded up by the SS following the invasion of Britain. Vera Brittain wrote about the early days of the war and her experiences as a London air raid warden in her book *England's Hour*, published in 1941:

We go out again into the area on a patrol of the public shelters. The Chief Post Warden accompanies us, wheeling his bicycle; in peace-time he is a glazier by profession, and was severely wounded in the War of 1914. Like his colleagues he wears an informal navy blue uniform, resembling a workman's dungarees. When the sirens go he mounts his bicycle and rides round the district, opening the locked shelters, and unlocking the First Aid apparatus and the shovels for dealing with incendiary bombs. If it is not locked up, this equipment provided by the locality for the public benefit, is invariably stolen. The thieves are as difficult to detect as the slatterns who leave the shelters littered with newspapers or the greasy wrappings of their fish-and-chips.

These surface shelters, built of brick and roofed with concrete, are reported to withstand any catastrophe but a direct hit from a bomb. They are said to be impervious to bullets and splinters, and the blast from an explosion may rock but will not shatter them. Each thick squat building has an alternative exit filled in with sheet-iron or loose bricks which can easily be removed. A dim electric bulb provides illumination. If the raid destroys the local supply of electricity, a lamp padlocked to the ceiling will provide light from its separate battery. Before the London raids have become severe, these shelters are popular owing to the sound-proof material which shuts out the noise of anti-aircraft barrage and distant bombs. Later, when several direct hits have shown that they may become death-traps which increase the number of casualties, a widespread agitation for deep shelters will arise, and London's poorer population will invade the Tubes. Most of the surface shelters are built, or adapted, as annexes to public buildings; one adjoins a church and another a convent; a third is a public laundry reinforced with iron and concrete. The district is humble, with a mainly working-class population inhabiting small two-storey houses without basements or garden shelters. It is for householders who possess neither Anderson steel shelters nor basements, that communal brick build-ings are now provided. Even when empty, their limited ventilation and their combined smell of concrete, new brick and Jeyes' Fluid makes them stuffy and close. When the public are in occupation, the atmosphere almost solidifies.

So far the residents of the small houses have taken to the shelters like foxes to their lairs. They have adopted them so effectively that they now camp there regularly with their blankets and pillows, rather than get up from a warm bed and emerge into the night when the siren goes.

'There's a whole set of social distinctions grown up in these shelters,' my friend the Warden tells me. 'The mutual exclusiveness of members at Yorkshire Luncheon Clubs is nothing to this. One group will refuse to enter the same shelter as another from their street. Then there are the quiet ones who won't share the shelter with children, and the Bright Young Things who play cards or darts and don't want elderly people. One old man regards a small communal shelter as his personal property; he sits there in his arm-chair and refuses to let anyone else come in.

Fifteen-year-old Clifford Brownbill lived with his parents at Sheerness in Kent and worked at a local glass factory. His diary for 6 September 1940 tells of raids on oil storage tanks at Thames Haven and reflects the excitement many people – of all ages – commonly felt watching air battles between the RAF and the Luftwaffe:

6th September
Here is a commentary of a fierce fight.

The warning was given and a few minutes later Gerry [Jerry – slang for Germans] arrived, the enemy planes were flying towards Chatham then our fighters tore across the sky and went for them hell for leather. I can hear our fighters zooming down and giving the enemy bursts of machine gun fire, they are coming back this way now, I can see them – there's machines everywhere. It looks as though the German formations have been split up.

I've got my eye on three machines. Oh! There go the machine guns again, a pilot of one of the planes has baled out while his plane careers off from the other two and disappears behind the clouds, smoke pouring from its tail. The parachute is dropping lower, it looks as if it's going to land in the sea. I can see the pilot on the end. Hallo sounds like another formation coming over, yes there they are 12 of them travelling towards London. There's a huge column of smoke rising from the direction of Thames Haven, they must have set the oil tanks on fire again. It was on fire last night. I went up the hill and had a look at it through Dick's glasses; the flames were terrific lighting up the whole of Sheerness and Q'boro [Queenborough]. This is the third time the tanks have been on fire in two days. Went up the hill, while up there the searchlights sprang up in the distance, a few minutes later off went the sirens, they were here again.

Letters were the main means of communication. Elizabeth Belsey was living at the family home in Keston, Kent, from where she wrote frequently to her husband, Lt John Belsey, serving with the Royal Artillery at Thames Ditton:

Fri Sept 6th 1940
Beloved
Here is your cheque-book and £ note – God knows when you will get them with the Post in the state it is. We got delayed and there were incendiary bombs here yesterday morning: afterwards the buses did not run beyond the Mark, and there were No Entry notices at the end of F Drive and Fishponds Road. Terrific explosion went off somewhere near in the evening. Crying scandal about the sirens last night: all-clear sounded at 5, when the sky was still swarming with German planes and searchlights. As soon as all was clear, the warning went again. I heard a

lot of nasty bumps in the night and I sweated with terror and slept very little.

As the autumn came, weather conditions in the Channel made a German invasion near-impossible. The RAF still controlled the air. Even if an initial invasion force crossed into England, it could not be kept supplied by sea. The Royal Navy and the RAF continued their battles but the Luftwaffe's commanders now turned their attention to the concentrated bombing of civilians in the cities. The immediate cause of this change in target was retaliation for the RAF bombing of Tempelhof, a suburb of Berlin, on 25 August 1940 – itself in retaliation for the Luftwaffe's earlier attack on Croydon on 15 August.

THE LONDON BLITZ

In a speech on 4 September 1940, Hitler criticised British forces for bombing Berlin. He told the German people, 'We shall now give a reply, night for night, and with increasing force ... If they declare that they will attack our cities on a large scale, we will erase theirs!'

Winston Churchill was now prime minister of Britain. Remembering the cheering crowds that had greeted Chamberlain after the Munich Agreement, Hitler thought that Winston Churchill wanted war with Germany, but the British people did not. Hitler believed that that British civilians would be demoralised by air raids on their towns and cities, and would put pressure on the British government to seek peace. In fact, the opposite was true: a key effect of the Blitz was to galvanise public opinion in Britain against Germany and in support of the war.

Two days later Hitler's threat became reality. In the official record of civil defence services, Terrence O'Brien described the first major raid on London:

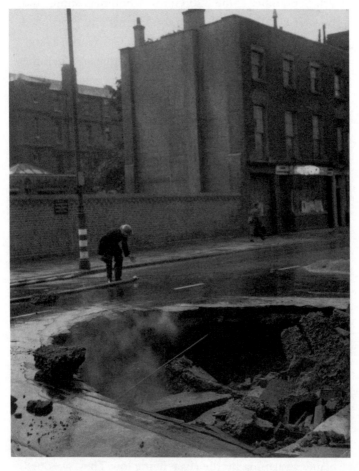

Somewhere in south-west London, after a raid, a fireman picks up a hose.
A high-explosive bomb has made a huge crater in the road. Gas, water and
electricity supplies were often disrupted for weeks after raids and roads
were blocked to most vehicles.

Between five and six o'clock on the evening of Saturday, 7th September some 320 German bombers supported by over 600 fighters flew up the Thames and proceeded to bomb Woolwich Arsenal, Beckton Gas Works, a large number of docks, West Ham power station, and then the City, Westminster and Kensington. They succeeded in causing a serious fire situation in the docks. An area of about 1½ miles between the North Woolwich Road and the Thames was almost destroyed, and the population of Silvertown was surrounded by fire and had to be evacuated by water.

This attack became known as Black Saturday.

Sir Aylmer Firebrace, later Chief of Staff of the National Fire Service, described the attack on the London docks:

The Surrey Commercial Docks, which lie to the right and rear of the plane, had been attacked simultaneously with those north of the River. Here are situated many basins, and vast stores of soft woods, mostly imported from the Baltic.

Shortly after five o'clock in the afternoon, the raid warning having been received a few minutes previously, a fireman, on duty at the top of the drill tower of the nearby Pageants Wharf Fire Station, reported a mass of planes swarming up the river, flying low. They swooped at once for the timber, there was never any doubt as to their objective. The dock area was immediately bespattered with incendiary bombs, with here and there a few high explosives and an occasional container of fuel oil, dropped to intensify the flames.

The vast area of some two hundred and fifty acres, containing thousands of standards of timber, including a lot of pitch pine and other resinous woods stored in sheds and on open ground, burst into flame. Incendiary bombs ignited the built-up deck cargoes of the many ships in the docks ... They lodged, burning, in inaccessible places in the huge piles of timber stacked twenty feet high; they fired the carpet of tindery wood chips, which had accumulated on the timber storage foundations, so spreading the fire with the rapidity of flashing gunpowder. In a very short time the heat was so intense that even the wood paving blocks in the roads were burning. A tempestuous roaring sea of fire, increasing in violence every minute, stormed its way into the heavens.

The Fire Officer, faced with this inferno and waiting impatiently for bulk reinforcements, may be excused a lapse from standard phraseology when he sent an exasperated message: 'Send all the bloody pumps you've got; the whole bloody world's on fire!' As far as could be seen, it was.

Firemen drenched the timber stacks with water, but, the moment they moved their jets to a new area, the soused wood steamed, dried, and once more burst into flame. Four auxiliary fire stations were engulfed and obliterated. Pumps became surrounded by fire and had to be abandoned, their crews only just making their escape in time. On the river bank, people were in imminent danger of being driven into the water by the flames, and had to be evacuated by boat. Those cut off by fire at South Wharf, which lies to the east of the dock area, sought refuge in a barge; with difficulty it was towed to safety by a fire boat, nosing its nightmare way between groups of moored small craft, most of them alight, and some burning furiously.

Forty-two huge fires were now raging; one was being fought with three hundred pumps and another required one hundred and thirty. Reinforcements poured in, some eventually coming from as far afield as Birmingham and Bristol. Throughout the frightful night Pageants Wharf Fire Station remained in action and became the focus for the direction of operations. Firewomen on duty here, well led by their woman officer, stuck to their job and put out fires threatening to destroy their building. They established a well-organized dressing station for the many firemen, some smoke blind, others in great pain from sparks from the burning wood having lodged in their eyes, who came in from the fire ground. For several weeks the firewomen were to be the only representatives of their sex in this neighbourhood; all others had been evacuated.

Meanwhile, in Woolwich:

Another big conflagration area created by the attack of 7th–8th September, 1940, was in the territory in which Woolwich Arsenal stands. Here land firemen and the crews of fire boats had to face the additional dangers of exploding ammunition. Projectiles from burning dumps of 'fixed' ammunition hurtled through the air turning base over nose in their flight, threatening fire boats and land fire engines impartially. Fire mains soon went out of action, and fires had to be fought with water obtained from the many dykes and ditches that abound in the Arsenal.

A message was received by the L.F.B. control stating that half a square mile of buildings containing H.E. shells was well alight, and the fire liable to spread to a large magazine. All fires must eventually go out; but strenuous efforts were required before this one conformed to the general rule.

The Thames as it flowed through the fire-ravaged docklands was experiencing the wildest night in its history. Along the south bank there was an unbroken wall of flame a thousand yards long. The fire blew half-way across the river, and such passing shipping as there was had to keep well over towards the north side, three hundred yards away. Even then some vessels could not face the heat and turned back; those that went on had their paint badly blistered.

More than sixty craft were sunk or destroyed on the river during this night of 7th–8th September. Numerous blazing barges, a number of them laden with inflammable copra (the inside of coconuts), their moorings having been burnt through, drifted down the river with the tide, threatening riverside wharves; they were to be borne back, still blazing, when the flood tide made.

Half a dozen London fire boats which had been at the Thames Haven oil tank fires were ordered back to London to join in the battle. Here is how the officer in charge afterwards described the journey: 'We kept close formation until we reached Woolwich, and then we saw an extraordinary spectacle. There was nothing but fire ahead, apparently stretching right across the river and burning on both its banks. We seemed to be entering a tunnel of fire – no break in it anywhere. All the usual land marks were obliterated by walls of flame. Burning barges drifted past. For many hours no contact with the shore was possible. We did what we could where we could as we slowly worked our way up river.

At one time we were just getting into position to fight a fire in a large warehouse when the whole of the riverside front collapsed into the water with a mighty splash. The contents of the building, bags of beans, pouring into the river made a sound like a tropical rain storm. Soon after, we were surprised to see two firemen and three firewomen picking their way along the shore in the direction of Southwark Bridge; they told us they had been cut off in a control room for several hours. They had undoubtedly had a rough time of it, but did not seem unduly perturbed.

This huge assault was very much concentrated around the riverside areas of London's East End. Other parts of London slowly began to hear of the attack. In *Westminster in War*, William Sansom wrote:

Towards six o'clock the fiction of unease became fact, the man on the street learnt that something had been happening in the East End, something more significant than the ordinary tidings brought by the siren – and Report Centres and other official quarters knew that at last the Luftwaffe had struck hard, there and then, that afternoon, at London proper. The docks were ablaze. And as the sun set, those in the East End streets grew conscious of the unbelievable, for the sunset occurred not only in the accustomed west near Putney and Willesden, but also incredibly in the West over St Paul's and where the City of London was held to lie. That was curious enough – but when the western skies had grown already dark the

fierce red glow of the sky in the East stuck harshly fast
and there was seen for the first time that black London
roofscape silhouetted against what was to become a
monotonously copper-orange sky. So in Westminster they
knew and they could see that something was happening
to the East. There was still prevalent the concept of special
targets for raiding bombers. A line of imagined strategy
was drawn up between the East and the West. The sky was
lit up, fearsomely – but there was not the expected massed
gunfire. So that, for Westminster, although the night began
more tensely indeed than others, it was yet without action,
without the feeling in fact of being attacked. Things were
unusual, but there was yet no climax.

This was only the beginning, as Terrence O'Brien wrote:

At 8.10 p.m. some 250 bombers resumed the attack, which
was maintained until 1.30 on Sunday morning. They
caused 9 conflagrations, 59 large fires and nearly 1,000
lesser fires. Three main-line railway termini were put out
of action, and 430 persons killed and some 1,600 seriously
injured. After the fire brigades had spent all day in an effort
to deprive the enemy of illumination, some 200 bombers
returned at 7.30 in the evening to carry on the assault.
During this second night a further 412 persons were killed
and 747 seriously injured, and damage included the temporary stoppage of every railway line to the south.

In Westminster, William Sansom noted that:

just after eleven o'clock, the first high explosives fell –
a stick of five bombs in the vicinity of Victoria Station

and Victoria Street. People were killed. People were wounded. The powdered smell of smashed plaster and brick poisoned the air for the first time. Glass, illimitable, spread itself across the pavements and over the road – it seemed to lie two or three inches thick. The peace was shattered, and the machine of defence went into action for its first real blooding.

It was an unlucky time – the public houses had just closed. Many people were out just then on the pavements, for at the end of the Vauxhall Bridge Road there was busying of late-night trams and buses. The iron replica of Big Ben stood then above a scene of stunned disaster and wounding, cries were heard from the neighbouring street, and in the great darkened railway station itself there occurred particular trouble. To this, then, came the ambulances and rescue parties for their first incident. The ambulance and stretcher parties were needed most; it was an open street affair; complicated rescue work was not called for. But all who drove there saw their first casualties. This first sight of blood and wounding is an experience sharp in its emotional effect, often physically affecting. People react, of course, according to their nature. Coldly in some, warmly in others. One girl ambulance driver, for instance, was sometimes physically sick back at the Depot after her night's work was done; she was able to hold on during the moments of needed action, but on relaxing afterwards was overcome with a delayed physical nausea. Others, at the other end of the scale, felt nothing, neither horror nor pity – yet underwent through this very coolness a mental disaffection, a self-condemnation for the lack of what they wished could be a capacity for pity.

That night several raiders drove high over Westminster and across farther west. They dropped in all about a dozen high explosive in the City's area. In retrospect, and relatively to the greater raids to come, this was small stuff, a peppering. They were small bombs, two weighing only fifty kilos. But each night, and each of those early nights in particular, must be regarded as a microcosm, a period of anxiety contained within itself and related only to the experience of the moment. It happened that of those dozen bombs, four hit Victoria Station. This, with the news of the fairly accurate firing of the East End docks, suggested at the time that special targets could be accurately selected. It was unfortunate, too, that of the other damage, important gas mains in Smith Square suffered, and even more disastrously a key 6,000 volt high tension electrical cable. This twin exposure of the vulnerability of under-street utility lines brought thus its early lesson to the repair services involved. The Gas Company learnt the meaning of broken pipes and thick London clay sogging any immediate chances of clean repair; and for the electricians in this case it was a more severe lesson, because of all the places in the City this was among the worst where a bomb could have dropped – it disturbed the main run of cables from a Bulk Supply Station bearing electricity bound for Whitehall. This bomb was of a delayed action type. It penetrated beneath the cables and lay there quiet. the supply company's emergency staff inspected the trouble – and then not long after the bomb exploded, damaging no fewer than twenty-six cables and destroying joints along the line. Cables were stretched and twisted and broken and tied into nightmare knots – but several remained alive – it gave evidence of the general toughness and resistance to damage of such cables even in these circumstances of phenomenal breakage.

So the next day, a Sunday, saw the various repair services go into action for the first time. The first surveys of damage were made, the first clearing of the streets and the first small traffic diversions. Meanwhile the skies to the south traced with white trails of fleece their dog-fights. German squadrons drove towards London – but Fighter Command fought a successful battle of interception. No bombs fell. Until nightfall. Then, between seven and eight o'clock a force of some two hundred bombers flew in to stir up the many great conflagrations still burning along the eastern docksides. And as before, some of these Heinkels and Dorniers came across and dropped a scattering of incendiaries and explosives in the Westminster City area.

In the early part of the night only incendiaries were dropped; they caused a few fires, but none serious. Then, in accordance with the contemporary German tactic of spreading their fires with explosives, the heavier bombs began to fall. This time the aim was more dispersed – bombs fell from the Covent Garden area to Hyde Park, Pimlico and Exhibition Road, covering thus a vague line inland from the Thames.

Among the more known buildings hit were the stables of the Cavalry at Knightsbridge Barracks, and the Royal Courts of Justice; a delayed action bomb fell in the grounds of Buckingham Palace.

The Southern Railway suffered again with a direct hit on the bridge in Grosvenor Road. However, the most important incidents of the night were experienced in more populated areas – in Neal Street for instance, where a high explosive bomb hit one of the wholesale fruit premises in this vicinity of Covent Garden. It was a grave incident, and here the Heavy Rescue parties first showed their mettle. They were faced with a building of several stories collapsed completely and blocking the narrow street into which it had fallen. People were known to have been on the upper floors. To make matters worse, a large fire developed next door and rescue work was impeded, drenched, sodden by water from the fire-hoses. Overhanging debris was dangerously insecure and of great weight. In soaking rubble and with the firelight flaring over a street confused with the litter of vegetables and water and hoses and bricks and timber – in such conditions the rescue workers picked among the breeze blocks of the devastated building and extricated the dead and the wounded.

There was another danger that complicated the clear-up:

Two important bombs fell in Shelton Street on the Holborn boundary and in Sussex Street. Both were of the delayed action type, and they gave the police and wardens their first experience of evacuation on a large scale. The Sussex Street bomb sent as many as two hundred people from their homes to the neighbouring Rest Centres, two school buildings held in readiness for the homeless.

Out in Kent, Elizabeth Belsey heard the planes rumble overhead to London, where her husband John was stationed with the Royal Artillery:

Sunday September 8th 1940

My darling

I hope for a letter from you tomorrow and will answer it, but meanwhile I send you a note to let you know we are all well, in spite of the ghastly blitz that London got last night.

We heard the planes at 8.30 (followed by the sirens), and then there was scarcely a moment's silence till the all-clear at 5. I had some nasty frights and did not sleep at all: we were shaken a bit but no harm done here.

John Belsey wrote back the same day:

Sunday 8th September 1940

My darling Girl

I am now to be a member of the armed party who run around in a lorry during an air raid looking for (with intent to capture) accidental or deliberate Nazi parachutists, but this is a spare time job and not my vocation.

How are you bearing up in these appalling air raids? Please, my darling, do not get too frightened and do not get damaged, and guard my lovely Charlotte.

It was terrible last night. We were up for nine hours, and the sky was lit by the most lurid glow from the tremendous fires in London. I watched the flames and the planes and the guns and I thought of you and had a terrible feeling that you were in danger. Please, my darling, do not get hurt. Please keep alive for me to come back to you, to love you, and look after you, and see my beautiful baby again. I will keep myself safe for you.

I am now living without sleep and I suppose you are too my darling and that is much worse. As I do practically no work, it doesn't matter so much, but a peaceful night now seems too beautiful and remote to be considered ...

Daylight showed the extent of the damage to the docks. Sir Aylmer Firebrace wrote:

Of the million and a half tons of soft wood timber concentrated in the Surrey Commercial Docks, four-fifths was destroyed. Daylight, so longed for by firemen on a big job, was to reveal a smoking wilderness; huge warehouses stood gutted; ships, which only a few hours previously had been discharging their cargoes, now lay, some on fire, some torn by blast, some sunk with only parts of their funnels and superstructure showing above the water.

For months the fire service had been seen by an increasing number of the public as a soft option; firemen were spat at in the street and auxiliary firemen in particular were called 'army dodgers'. Next morning the pumps returned to their stations carrying the 'army dodgers', slumped down with exhaustion, filthy with smoke, who were cheered all along the roads. Michael Wassey, a London AFS man wrote; 'In the bar of a certain hotel the yellow-haired barmaid always ignored my uniform and served every customer before me. It was typical of the public's reaction to the AFS.' And then, after 7 September 1940; 'Scum was transferred into cream overnight ... The yellow-haired barmaid has served me first ever since.'

While the firemen and women were now treated as heroes, public anger found a new target; there seemed to have been no anti-aircraft fire against the raiders. The guns had been sited near the coast, to be able to shoot at the

enemy on their way in and out, but the absence of anti-
aircraft fire over the capital was bad for morale.

Terrence O'Brien explained: 'On these and the next
few nights it seemed to the London public that the enemy
bombers could roam at will and attack where they chose
without any effective opposition. But on 11th September
our anti-aircraft barrage suddenly roared out, causing the
citizens to cheer in the streets.'

Interviewed by Mass Observation shortly after, Nita
Marcus, a 27-year-old ambulance driver in Lewisham,
south London, said:

We have started using the phrase 'since the war started'
meaning since Saturday afternoon when the great raid
set the whole skyline ablaze; all the hilltops here (which
gives a fine view of the Thames and dockside and half
of London) were covered with sightseers between the
first raid and the second. Bombs first dropped in this district on Friday, just a few – knocking over a church, and
upsetting our phone at the station, which is still out of
order after 3 days so that we have to work through the
nearest Warden's Post. Saturday Muriel's (the sister now
in Canada) house was bombed, which she let earlier in
the year, when she moved to Worthing. I went to look at
it yesterday and found her husband standing amongst the
ruins, just staring, unable to take himself away. Another
girl at the station still has a cousin in the cellar of a collapsed house – whether alive or dead no-one knows, but
they got a dog out alive.

All our stations round here sent out ambulances.
One of ours came back with an epic story. Manned by
Matthewman, (a little, elderly, charming creature) and

Georgie (who has a sagging chin and vacant expression) it went down to Surrey Docks, through flames meeting from each side of the road (where our next ambulance two minutes later could not get through) and picked up 5 casualties, including one woman who had just had a baby. Sparks and fragments kept falling on them – they beat them off their trousers and stamped out the ropes that hold the back curtains and came back another way past a wall that collapsed behind them.

London was bombed every day throughout the rest of September and October 1940. General Sir Frederick Pile, who led Anti-Aircraft Command throughout the war, later described anti-aircraft's initial efforts as 'appalling … we seemed as far as ever from solving the great problem of the night raider'. Night fighters and night interception methods were still, embryonic. He ordered guns from all over the country to London, and instructed them on 11 September to 'fire every available round …Their fire was mostly ineffectual, but the sound of the local guns opening up gave a huge morale boost to the shelterers.'

The bombers concentrated on the City area and the East End, the River Thames providing a shining silver path to guide them. Will, an ARP warden in east London, was a schoolteacher in Leytonstone in peacetime. He wrote to his brother and sister-in-law in Abergavenny, Wales, about the first week of the Blitz on London:

Leytonstone E 11 Wed. Sept. 18th [1940] Dear Alb. & Bett, Now that I have a few minutes to spare I thought you might like to have a dispatch from one of England's many war fronts – London.

You know already that we've been getting it hot &
strong up here ever since I've been back. Each night
there is a raid warning lasting for 8 hours or more –
mostly about 9 hrs, although last night it was 9 hrs 53
mins (from 8.07 pm – 6 am) with another warning at
7 am and three more since. Most days we get five or
more warnings although only once or twice a day perhaps do we see an air battle. One is, in fact, going on
above us now. We've had two long day-warnings lately –
one last Friday from 8.55 am – 2 pm & one on Monday
from 2.15 pm – 6 pm. School is a farce, as only half or less
of the boys attend & we spend our time in the corridors
which are our shelters. During these all-night raids we
actually get heavy gunfire & planes overhead for 8 or 9
hrs. Sometimes there's a lull for half hr. after the warning
is given, before the show starts. Sometimes – most often,
the guns and sirens go together. The last ½ hour before
the 'all clear' is usually quiet.

I can't possibly tell you of the number of bombs which
have fallen say within 1 mile or 1½ miles of this house –
while Stratford, Bow, Plaistow etc are terribly smashed
up. I told you, I think, of a bomb in Grove Green Rd. &
one on a shelter in Forest Drive West. Later we had an
aerial torpedo in Hainault Rd right at the end of our
street. Bombs fell on a number of shops in Leytonstone
High Rd & smashed 4 of them to mere rubble. Another
bomb fell in the churchyard opposite Woolworths. Last
Saturday night was the worst. An aerial torpedo landed
directly on houses in Forest Drive West. Five were blown
to pieces – not a stick of furniture even could be seen –
only piles of earth, loose bricks & beams of timber.
Eleven bodies have been recovered & they think there

are still more to be found. Forty houses around (including the one whose shelter was hit the previous week) have been rendered uninhabitable & scores more in the street behind have had windows, doors, chimneys etc destroyed. Mr. B— lives 4 doors away & their house is badly damaged. The noise of that torpedo falling was terrifying – like a mighty rushing wind. I was lying awake in the bed & it seemed to be coming straight for us. The explosion made the whole house rock. 30 secs. later another aerial torpedo came and wiped out the United Dairies factory, a shop & two houses in Hainault Rd. That's the second aerial torpedo within 300 yds in Hainault Rd. A school has been hit & the workhouse in Union Rd. was struck by another aerial torpedo & several wards demolished. They are still digging for bodies.

These aerial torpedoes weigh about 1,800 lbs to 1 ton. The noise of gunfire, the whistle of shrapnel & the scream of falling bombs is appalling. Every few moments a plane or group of planes come nearer and nearer – the local guns blaze away & then a few bombs – sometimes near – sometimes further off. Sleep is impossible.

Last Monday I was put on duty as a warden for the first time since I've been back. My patrol is from the corner of Cavendish Drive down past our house to the bottom and up Scarborough Rd. I report when a warning comes. The post is about 150 yds down Cavendish Drive. Nothing had happened in our sector & I was told it was easy. The siren went on Monday at 10 minutes to eight in the evening. I reported at the post. The guns were already blazing away & planes were overhead. I walked back to the house – dodging into doorways when I heard shrapnel falling. I put on my mac & then it came – a 'Molotov basket' of 50 incendiary bombs on our street, a few on the flats behind us & a number on the railway embankment behind Mrs. S—'s. Some fell on Norlington School which is just across the line. I rushed out and blew my whistle to summon the wardens (3 of them) who were standing by. The whole street seemed ablaze with white magnesium glare. There were 10 fires between our house & the post. [Number] 94 escaped, but two fell three doors away.

I tackled one which was blazing under a front window and got it out quickly. Then the woman screamed out that one had fallen on a shed full of timber in her back garden & was blazing away. I rushed through the house & tackled the bomb with sand. Then I put out the blaze in the shed with buckets of water. The other wardens were working singly on other fires down their end of the street. Norlington School was blazing furiously & the Magnet Laundry next door. The Brigades were at work there.

The wardens of the next post were dealing with the fires in the flats. The remaining fires in Cavendish Drive we put out working together on stirrup pumps. One fire in an unoccupied house (No. 23) we did not notice for some time & it had got going. However we got them all out in really good time & with very little damage considering. The A.F.S. etc. were attending to the blazing school & Jerry was using it as a landmark & letting drop salvo after salvo of high explosive & the guns were blazing furiously. It was like hell let loose. I found several unexploded (or unignited to be exact – they don't explode) incendiary bombs which I had to carry away and bury in buckets of sand. Finally we mopped our begrimed faces

& went to the post to write the report that all was in hand. Jerry was still pasting us. I came out on patrol again to make sure that none of the fires had restarted & 2 of the wardens came out with me. We had just left the post & there came the whistle of a bomb overhead – we dropped flat to the ground & it landed on the doorstep of 50 Cavendish Drive – only 25–30 yds from where we were lying. For a second or so I hardly realized I was alive. Then I ran to the house and plunged in to see if anyone was in there or hurt – it was like going into a fog with smoke and dust. Wreckage was all over the place. I searched the house and found only a dog shut up in the kitchenette & unhurt. Later we found that the people had gone to a public shelter for the first time that night. The front of that house and the neighbouring ones were smashed up & windows were broken over 100 yds away. When I saw the chunks of masonry & bits of iron railings that must have flown over our heads as we lay on the ground, I realized how lucky I was. Actually it was only a small bomb – a 25 or 50 lb one – Had it been larger, I might not have been writing this. To our amazement an 'all clear' went about 3 am but it was too good to be true. Jerry was back in an hour, pasting us again. He finally packed up just before 6 am. I had to look after the debris & watch there until daylight. When I got home I was more tired and worn out than I've ever been before. A neighbour brought me a cup of tea while I was on duty & Mrs. S—, kind soul, gave me breakfast when I came off duty about 7 am. There was another warning at 8 am & then I had to collect the unspent incendiary bombs and take them to A.R.P. Headquarters (I wish I kept a bomb now, as a souvenir). A phone message came through that a time-bomb was buried outside our school & that the area was evacuated. When I reached A.R.P. headquarters I was sent with another warden to examine certain places where it was thought time bombs had fallen. As a matter of fact we found none. It was 4 pm before I got a chance to sleep yesterday. It has been found out that the supposed time-bomb near our school was really a dud A.A. shell, so school is open today. I have rescued the fins of the first German incendiary bomb which I put out, as a souvenir. The bombs that fell on Monday night have done damage all over the place. Over 70 bombs – incendiaries and high explosives – are reported to have fallen in Leytonstone on that one night. Last night I was off duty – standing by in case of more incidents. I have put a mattress in the cupboard under the stairs & I lie there fully dressed with tin hat, torch, whistle etc. to hand. There was very heavy gunfire last night & I heard some bombs drop, but not very near. The Germans are dropping land-mines by parachute – one went off at the Bell, Walthamstow & rendered 100 houses uninhabitable, and, wonderful to say, killed only 1 person.

I must confess that the long weary hours of waiting and listening through the night, quite alone in the house with not a soul to talk to, were very trying, but I am profoundly glad that Rube and the kiddies are away. This is no place for women and children. Many folk have packed up and left here recently, & I don't blame them. This dislocation of traffic has made it very difficult for business folk & often they have to walk long distances. This bombing has shown the disadvantages of trolley buses compared with buses. Once the trolley bus route has been hit, the route is blocked as trolley buses can't go round sideways. Nearly all the main line termini are closed & many suburban stations. However the biggest nuisance is the inability to shop, get a bath, haircut or go to church without being disturbed by the raids. We have had no [domestic] gas for the last fortnight & are not likely to get any for the duration. You can't get any hot stuff in Lyons etc in Leytonstone – not even tea, & often there is no food as the motor deliveries are held up. Tea can be got at Baker's Arms because they are on a different gas system.

Well, that's enough about war. How are you getting on? I suppose you are settling in your new home & I hope you are very happy there. Are you having much raid trouble? Drop me a line when you get time – I know you are busy now. Give my love to Brian & Sheila. Boys up here no longer collect cigarette pictures – they collect shell fragments. There's plenty of it about the streets. If Brian would like a piece I'll send him some.

Now I must ring off, as I'm on duty tonight. It's 6 pm now – I've been writing this letter between whiles.

Look after yourselves. Lots of love,

Will XXXXXXXXXXXXXXXXX

Postal services were disrupted but letters were still getting through. Elizabeth Belsey wrote:

Wed Sept 11th 3.20 pm

My darling boy

It was a delight to get your letter this morning at break-fast. I sent you a small parcel with a letter yesterday but I feel I must answer you with another. The sirens have just blown off for the second time today: let's hope as little happens now as this morning. Mother and Jeremy are out: I hope they will find proper cover. On Monday night I was quite sleepless and terrified, with the result that last night, after feeding Charlotte, I fell into bed and slept like a log until 6, waking momentarily when the all-clear went at 4.45. I hope I shall be able to again tonight. I often think of you, my darling, out in a cold trench when I am warm in bed. Please try to sleep there, if it is humanly possible. I hope nothing too bad has occurred near you. We are all right: it's my belief that we are safer than we were – that they are now concentrating on Central London. We had four warnings yesterday, but heard nothing. It is dreadful to think of what is happening in London: the pictures in the papers make me feel sick. Sally says it is now quite difficult to get about London with any certainty. She will probably have to stay in London as the raids get earlier and earlier in starting. Jeremy has fixed a wire-netting frame in the landing window, to catch glass. He went to the Admiralty yesterday, and will probably do his advanced engineering course at Greenwich, but for the present is on leave.

You must not worry about me, sweetheart; I am quite well and feel much better than I did at first. I too had fears that you were in danger on Saturday night – but it seems we were both wrong! I will keep alive and well for you to come home to, and I will take care of my precious baby for you too. I would die for her if necessary, though it is unlikely that anything which killed me would not kill her too, as we are never far apart. You too must take care of yourself for me and her, as I do not know how I could endure your loss. I pray that all or none of us may survive this war; but not one or two …

8 pm

Sally has just got home, exhausted. Holborn is the only
station functioning between London and Bromley, and
the crush is fearful. The sirens have not blown yet, but
I expect them to any minute. I am reading Wuthering
Heights again and I find I enjoy it as much as ever before.
This is strange for though I still think it one of the world's
greatest novels, it is wild and formless and unrealistic. But
perhaps that is why I enjoy it now – because it echoes my
state of mind. It is a restless book and gives one no peace,
even though it deals with life in a remote Yorkshire district a hundred and fifty years ago. Though it is unrealistic
it is not unreal; while reading it, one lives in it – more so,
I think, than in any other book I know. Through all its
improbability, it convinces one of its truth.

On the whole, I think the nineteenth-century novel
should make good wartime reading (damn sirens just
going): its very size and ponderability make it somehow
comforting. I will stop this letter now and send it to you
in the morning. I had meant to catch tonight's post, but
it had to be written at intervals and I couldn't manage it.

Take care of yourself, my darling …

The guns are banging and banging; but I pray you may
have a passably good night.

With all my love Elizabeth

As the bombs fell, pre-war arguments over the provision
of shelters intensified. Public shelters were a major concern. These were essential in the built-up areas of London,
where few people had the room indoors or out to use the
domestic alternatives. Those that were built were often

badly constructed, and in London there were too few for the numbers needing them. Shelters adapted from existing buildings were often insanitary. During raids, people gathered in church halls, under railway arches and in cellars. On the first night of the Blitz, 10,000 people gathered in one cellar in the East End – twice its official capacity.

Doctors wrote to the *British Medical Journal*, warning that typhus and cholera epidemics would result from sending people into overcrowded, insanitary shelters, and by fractured sewage and water mains.

Within a week of the start of the Blitz, the government set up a committee under Sir John Horder, the most prominent doctor in Britain at that time. It was to investigate and make recommendations on health conditions in the public shelters. A few weeks into the Blitz, the BMJ reported:

> The worst 'shelter' of all seen in the East End was discovered under some railway arches, each arch accommodating from seventy to one hundred people. Here the only lavatory accommodation was a couple of buckets for the women; the men had to manage outside. There was not a single water tap under the whole of the arches; if the shelterers wanted a drink of water they had to bring it with them. The lighting also was very poor, the people supplementing it from candles. In wet weather the water percolated all over this shelter, and there was not a dry spot. The only help afforded was by the students of the London Hospital, who come every night to give whatever assistance they can, and by a local vicar who distributes cups of cocoa.

The intention was that ARP was organised so that those with expertise could quickly advise those on the ground.

However, another doctor, in the East End of London, writing anonymously to the *BMJ*, said that as the medical officer at an ARP first-aid post, he was under the control of six different groups:

> At present those people who are actually concerned in doing are hampered immensely by the bureaucratic-minded instead of being assisted by acknowledged experts with practical experience.

The public shelters highlighted the differences in social class – while those in the East End, the poorer part of the city, had too few shelters to go to, wealthier people, who had not left the city, were able to use deep shelters offered by the clubs and hotels of the West End.

Those in poorer and cramped housing often had no room for a Morrison shelter indoors and no garden for an Anderson outside.

Phil Piratin, leader of Stepney Council, was a member of the Communist Party, which had criticised the lack of public shelters since before the war. He recalled in his memoir, published in 1948, the direct action he led in the first week of the London Blitz to highlight the problems in London's East End:

> Many people were without shelter, and every evening there was a trek from Stepney to central and west London to take shelter in one of the basement shelters of the large buildings there. The next morning thousands of bleary-eyed Londoners were to be seen on the buses and trains coming back to east London from the West End. The contrast between the shelter conditions

for the rich and the poor called for exposure. This was
done. When the blitz had continued for some days, we
in Stepney took the initiative. One Saturday evening
we gathered some seventy people, among them a large
sprinkling of children, and we took them to the Savoy
Hotel. We had heard from building workers of the well-
constructed and luxurious shelter which had been built
for their guests. We decided that what was good enough
for the Savoy Hotel parasites was reasonably good
enough for Stepney workers and their families. We had
an idea that the hotel management would not see eye to
eye with this proposition, so we organised the 'invasion'
without their consent. In fact, there was some effort
to stop us, but it was only a matter of seconds before
we were downstairs, and the women and children
came streaming in afterwards. While the management
and their lackeys were filled with consternation, the
visitors from east London looked round in amazement. 'Shelters,' they said, 'why we'd love to live in such
places!' Structurally, the lower ground floor had been
strengthened with steel girders and by other means. But
the appearance of the place! There were three sections.
In each section there were cubicles. Each section was
decorated in a different colour, pink, blue and green.
All the bedding, all the linen, was, of course, the same
uniform colour. Armchairs and deck chairs were strewn
around ... We had earlier appointed our marshals to
take care of all our people. They immediately made
contact with the waiters, and asked for water and other
such provisions. The waiters were most helpful. We
were expecting trouble; we knew that the management
was not going to allow us to sit there, just so easily. After

a few minutes the police came. A plain-clothes officer said to me, 'What is it all about?' I explained. He said: 'We will have to get you out.' I said: 'O.K. – I'm curious to see what you do with the women and children.' (The blitz was on.) ...

The management was in a dilemma. They urged the police to throw us out. We were able to impress on the manager that any such attempt would meet with some opposition, and that some of his guests in the dining room were likely to be disturbed. The manager left. He agreed to ignore us; that was what we wanted. Then we settled down. The first thing the marshals did was to call for refreshments. Many of our people had sandwiches with them and we therefore asked one of the waiters to provide tea and bread and butter. The waiter explained that they never served tea and bread and butter, and in any case the minimum price for anything was 2s. 6d. We said to the waiter: 'We will pay you 2d. a cup of tea and 2d. a portion of bread and butter, the usual prices in a Lyons' restaurant.' Three or four of the waiters went into a huddle, with one in particular doing the talking. He was evidently convincing the others. How they convinced the chef and management, I do not know, but within a few minutes, along came the trolleys and the silver trays laden with pots of tea and bread and butter. The waiters were having the time of their lives. They were obviously neglecting their duties, standing around, chuckling and playing with the children. The next day this news was flashed across the world. The contrast was made in bold headlines between the terrible conditions of the shelters in Stepney and the luxury conditions of the shelters of West London.

The government was reluctant to allow people to take shelter in the Underground stations in London, fearing they might clog up the vitally important transport system, but people took matters into their own hands. Buying a ticket on the Circle line and staying the night became common practice. Efforts to prevent people from occupying Tube stations were brushed aside by other organised mass actions and by the large numbers of people going into stations in anticipation of raids. Unofficial queuing systems meant people – often children – would arrive early in the morning, as a Tube station opened, to occupy a space for the family when the raids came that night. Government fears that people would refuse to come out of the stations between raids proved baseless.

Sir John Horder's report into the shelters was written and implemented within weeks. Public air raid shelters of all kinds were sprayed liberally and frequently with disinfectant. Fears of epidemics subsided and although 'shelter cough' became a popular if vague medical term for a persistent cough, there were no outbreaks of more dangerous infectious diseases. The report also proposed and organised London Tube stations as shelters.

Soon nearly 150,000 people were using the Tube every night to shelter from the Blitz. Tickets were issued for regular berths and the Red Cross ran first-aid posts. By May 1941, over one million bunk beds had been fitted in Tube stations and other official public shelters, along with toilets and washing facilities. Some of the Tube stations without catering were served by a 'canteen train' service that passed though stations.

The government also ordered eight deep shelters for London, holding in total over 60,000 people – but they

Sheltering in Aldwych Underground station, November 1940. When the trains had finished running, the power was turned off to allow shelterers to sleep between the tracks.

were not completed until the end of 1942, long after the end of the Blitz.

American journalist Quentin Reynolds recorded a typical scene at Camden Town Tube station in his wartime publication *The Wounded Don't Cry*. London-based American journalists such as Reynolds greatly influenced public opinion in the USA. They were crucial in creating the propaganda emerging from the Blitz, of Britain as a plucky nation prepared to 'grin and bear it':

We climbed downstairs to the platform. The concrete stairs were crowded. You had to step over people.

The platform was packed with people lying on the concrete. Some were playing cards.

This is how thousands of families live at night in London – far under the ground. Usually the working man of the family arrives home about five-thirty. He'll find something hot in the stove being kept warm – if the gas main hasn't been destroyed. He'll find tea on the stove too. But his wife and children have long since left for the safety of the Tube. It is first come first served, and they went early.

When Pop finishes his meal he joins them. They've saved a place for him. It may be cold down there and the air sticky with the feel of hundreds of people packed closely together – but it's safe. He and his family accept their lot philosophically. This is a new world and they adapt themselves to it.

A man with an accordion came in and was greeted with friendly banter. He played Tomorrow is a Lovely Day, There'll Always be an England, and even the kids joined in the singing. Then he played the most popular song of the day, A Nightingale Sang in Berkeley Square. Several 'incidents' have occurred in Berkeley Square during the past month and the accordion player commemorated them by singing his version of the song, calling it A Screaming Bomb fell in Berkeley Square.

They all laughed at that. All but me. I live in Berkeley Square.

It was getting late now. The Underground dwellers impose a nine o'clock curfew on themselves. The accordion player pillowed his head on the accordion. A heavy quiet settled over the reclining forms.

The guns and the bombs seemed far away. A train pulled in. Those who were asleep never woke, for noise is so much part of our existence in London these nights that it is only quiet that disturbs us because it seems unnatural.

Away from the city centre, many people with their own gardens had an Anderson shelter. This was made from corrugated steel sheets bolted together and half buried in the ground. Earth was then piled on top. The standard Andersons were 4ft 6in wide and 6ft high, and could accommodate between four and six people, but could be adapted for up to ten people by adding extra corrugated panels. But they were often damp and inclined to flooding. J.L. Stevens, returned home after her convalescence to Hornchurch, Essex, recalled:

In early October 1940, our shelter filled with water and we were unable to use it anymore.

One evening at the end of October we were sitting in the kitchen – I was reading, my mother was heating milk on the gas cooker. There was an air raid on but there was nowhere else for us to go so we just stayed there. We heard the sound of a German plane and guns were firing at it. My father decided to go into the garden to see where it was and then came in to say it had been hit and was coming down.

He went to the front door to check its progress and as it came down it jettisoned its load of bombs and incendiaries. Unfortunately, as my father opened the front door a huge bomb exploded in front of our house. We did not hear the bomb coming – I remember a roaring sound and everything went dark; a hole appeared in the side and rear walls of our kitchen; my mother screamed and shouted for help and cried 'won't anyone save us?' (She was constantly reminded of this for many years – my father thought it a huge joke.)

My father, who was in the hall, shouted that the kitchen door was stuck and he would have to knock it down – by that time, hot and cold water from the fractured tanks had started pouring through the ceiling. The front door and stairs had been completely blown away. We crawled through the hole into the garden and my father said we would have to go into next door's shelter. We had to negotiate round two incendiaries on the garden path – my mother in her shocked state stepped over them and consequently set on fire her nightdress and burned her legs. A huge sheet of flame from igniting gas came through the hole from which we had crawled.

My father went off to review the situation and eventually came back with a rescue team, as unknown to us the bomb had fractured the main water pipe in the road and this was cascading everywhere.

My mother, who had also been scalded by the hot milk, had to be carried from the shelter. I was dressed only in pyjamas and slippers and by this time walking was difficult against the flow of water; it had also started to rain to add to our misery.

The damage to surrounding properties was considerable and the crater extended over two pavements, the road and our front garden right up to the front door. The boulders strewn around seemed enormous. An ambulance was summoned to take my mother to Oldchurch Hospital, Romford; this duly arrived but broke down on the way and it was two hours before she eventually got to the hospital. She was, in due course, awarded a War Pension.

My father left me in the care of neighbours, not knowing where to go while he went to a first aid post to get a head wound dressed. Later he found me in the public shelter near Elm Park station – I was very wet and bedraggled so he borrowed a blanket into which I wrapped myself and he dried my clothing over a paraffin stove.

In the morning we went to a church in North Street, Hornchurch, which was being used as a reception centre for homeless families. I was given a pair of trousers, a coat (very thin), jumper, shoes and socks.

My father was given £10 as an immediate clothing allowance and, I believe, £20 for furniture. As we had no home it hardly mattered. After five days we had to leave and my father arranged that we should stay with his two sisters who also lived in Hornchurch. (We slept on the floor for two months.)

We had been very worried about our canary who had been buried under the kitchen debris but he was eventually rescued by the demolition squad some three days later. Fortunately he had sufficient food and water and had sung all day so his exact location was known. The larder door had fallen over his cage and this had sheltered him from the elements and debris which were constantly falling down. He was taken to the home of a PDSA inspector and a week later my father and I went to collect him. On the way a German plane suddenly flew low along the road and started machine-gunning: my father pulled me to the side of the wall of a house for protection. Having only just been bombed this was a somewhat unnerving experience.

Each raid left unexploded bombs – some delayed action, some simply malfunctioning – across the cities. Now based in London, Henry Beckingham's life of enforced leisure was over:

We were now in the thick of the action – air raids every night and many during daylight hours. There was not time for leisure; we worked seven days a week from morning till late at night, and the only piece of equipment we had was a two-pin discharger … This company alone dealt with 470 UXBs during the last 14 days in September, therefore it can safely be assumed that they handled some 700 incidents in the month of September. Quite a staggering figure when one considers this company was responsible for the North of the Thames. No 23 BD Coy RE [Bomb Disposal Company Royal Engineers] was carrying out a similar role south of the river from their headquarters in Balham.

It shows the ferocity of the air raids when, in spite of the number dealt with in September, No 5 BD Coy had still 632 incidents on their books on 1st October.

His initial one-day training was supplemented by on-the-job experience. As he soon learned, most bombs did not sit conveniently on the surface:

One incident I will recall which will show the luck, or fate or whatever you will call it, which followed me around.

Having spent a number of days excavating for a UXB in the rear garden of a semi-detached house in Seven Kings' Road in Ilford, we eventually recovered the tail fins and knew the bomb to be a 250kg. This spurred us on to more frantic digging because we knew the bomb could not be very far away. At last we reached the filler cap of the bomb which needed more digging to uncover the fuse or fuses. Luck was not with us; the bomb had come to rest at an acute angle and the fusepocket or pockets were underneath.

It was decided to call it a day and to go back the following morning. You can imagine our sense of shock and horror when we arrived back the next day to find four houses all very badly damaged. The local residents informed us that the bomb had exploded one hour after we had left the scene. That was the fate or luck that repeated itself on other occasions.

One assumes that in all these incidents a clockwork delay fuse had been restarted due to the disturbance of the bomb. It was common for these fuses to stop with very little time left to run before they detonated. Thank heavens the ARP personnel always evacuated the area around an incident which kept fatalities to an absolute minimum.

On another occasion we were excavating for a bomb in the centre of Ilford when out of the blue a German plane swooped down upon us machine guns blazing as he roared past. I was in the excavation and the rest of our squad had taken shelter in nearby shop doorways. At this precise moment the floor of the excavation caved in, and that's all I can recall until much later when I regained consciousness and I was lying in a hospital bed in Ilford, with the worst headache I could ever recall. I again had been extremely lucky. During the raid a policeman and members of the BD squad who had been taking cover in the nearby shop doorways saw my head suddenly disappear; they dashed across the road and managed to get me out. I was unconscious having inhaled a good lungful of carbon monoxide gas, but luckily after a few days in hospital I was back in the unit and uncovering more UXBs.

The reason for the above incident was that a 50kg bomb had penetrated the earth before exploding. The force of the explosion had not been sufficient to break the surface of the roadway and thus form a crater, instead the explosion had created a sealed chamber, commonly known as a Camouflet. Subsequently orders were issued to the effect that anyone working on the excavation had to have a lifeline around his waist which was secured to a picket at ground level. This restriction on movement resulted in this order being generally ignored, unless there was an officer around.

Cecil Beaton regularly toured central London photographing the aftermath of raids for the Ministry of
Information, and he recorded people's reactions in his diary:

At the Natural History Museum the curator showed me
the wreckage. The Times, he complained, had minimized
the damage. Why, the herborium had been burnt out by
an incendiary bomb! And that was the centre of interest
of all the botanists of the world! Vitrines by the acre were
smashed to smithereens, the carcasses of pre-historic ani-
mals had gone to dust – and the force of an explosion
had caused a sheet of writing paper to cut a crack right
through a mahogany cupboard door ...

I went to Albemarle Street to see if the wax head I had
seen among the debris of a former hairdressing establishment was still there. As I arrived a demolition squad was
pulling down a large top-heavy facade. Whrump! The
cloud of black dust eventually settled. I clambered over
the rubble to find a new wax head lying, bald but smiling,
among the cracked mirrors, glass fragments and wreckage of the ladies' beauty shop. The men working on the
job were helpful, and when I asked one if he had seen
lately the head with golden hair flying wild, he said he
thought it could be unearthed. It was. The ghoulish head
was produced from a mound of rubbish, and I proceeded
to photograph it against the dreadful surroundings.

Suddenly the usual officious passer-by appeared. A little
man with ferret eyes and a pointed red nose. I must show
my papers. Yes, there was nothing wrong with the papers,
but it didn't say you could photograph those wax heads –
it wasn't right – the Ministry of Information would not

want to show anything like that. I explained that, in any case, my photographs had to be submitted to the censor. But the discontent had started and now gathered momentum. The newspaper seller, who before had been so blithe and friendly, became truculent and grumbled that he wouldn't let me leave the spot until a policeman appeared and proved that everything was in order. A plain-clothes man edged his way through the gathering crowd, and whispered that everything was straightforward but that the feelings of the people must be pacified.

It was some time before the constable appeared and I was escorted to the nearest police station. After a few telephone calls everything was put right, but the constable explained that I had done wrong in provoking the antagonism of the crowd and a record should be made of the case. This seemed a somewhat empty formality since all the records had been destroyed by last night's bomb.

Clifford Brownbill's diary of life in Sheerness records:

23rd September
Had just finished washing when the sirens sounded. Mum and dad were at the pictures but they came home just before six in time for the King's speech. While he was in the middle of his speech the all clear was sounded in London. We could hear it coming through on the wireless so I got myself ready to go out for I knew ours would not be long. The all clear went just as the King finished speaking and overhead formations of British fighters roared as if in salute when the National Anthem was being played.

9th October

All I seem to be doing nowadays is eating my dinner in the shelter. It is worth bringing your dinner ...

The alert is sounding while a German is overhead. They have been flying around for about fifteen minutes before the alert. It's the same old routine, a raider comes over, the searchlights try to pick him out while the guns blaze away at the sound of his engines. This raid is the longest of the war – 11 and a half hours.

The raids created new opportunities for crime and criminals. Looting from bombed houses was widespread. In the first eight weeks of the Blitz on London 390 cases of looting was reported to the police. On 9 November 1940, the first twenty cases of people accused of looting were heard at the Old Bailey. Of these, ten involved members of the Auxiliary Fire Service.

The Lord Mayor of London suggested that notices should be posted throughout the city, reminding the population that looting was punishable by hanging or shooting. However, the courts continued to treat this crime more leniently. When a gang of army deserters was convicted of looting in Kent, the judge handed down sentences ranging from five years' penal servitude to eight years' hard labour.

So many people were losing their homes during 1940 that officials of the local National Assistance Offices did not have enough time to check people's claims. This was made even more difficult when someone's identity card and ration book had also been destroyed during air raids.

By 1941 the government realised that it was paying out more than expected and suspected fraud was widespread.

Extra staff were brought in to make more detailed checks on the claims being made. One of the first to appear in court was Walter Handy, who was sent to prison for three years for falsely claiming he had been 'bombed out' (made homeless) nineteen times in five months.

During the first weeks of the war, cinemas, theatres and other public entertainment places had closed. The Government feared the mass casualties that would ensue if bombs fell on crowded spaces. Public opinion and the initial lack of enemy action forced a rethink and many re-opened. Some theatres and cinemas would continue during raids, posting a warning and asking people who wished to take shelter, to 'leave quietly'.

Once the raids began, Vera Brittain said:

In the theatres and concert halls, impromptu performances now follow the programmes to fill the time during six and seven-hour raids ...

After a few days, most people continue their occupations when the siren sounds; often, writing my book or dictating letters, I become so oblivious of the raid that when the 'All Clear' goes, I imagine it to be another warning. In some of the big stores, 'roof-spotters' now relay a running commentary to the customers taking shelter below. 'There's a puff of smoke in the North-West! ... Now there's nothing, so I'll put on a record.'

People complained of tiredness, rather than terror:

Already, if we are honest, we shall admit that we wake every morning with heads heavy and eyes dry from the interrupted night; that the daily sirens are beginning to challenge our powers of concentration with their insistent scream.

Commander Sir Aylmer Firebrace commented on the public reaction during raids:

It was not at all unusual for children to escape from shelters and join in the firefighting. During a particularly heavy attack on London, a pair of 'treasures' about ten years old were told somewhat sharply by a fire officer to get back into their shelter. The boys, however, wanted to remain to see the fun, and to lend a hand. One, having achieved a safe distance, shouted indignantly, 'T'ain't your bloody war, mister!'

Adults were little different.

Once, when a large gas main was alight in Kennington, a wide area was brilliantly illuminated. Notwithstanding that bombers were at that moment droning overhead, and would be likely to re-bomb the incident at any moment, hundreds of men, women and children emerged from their shelters to watch the sight. If there was excitement going, they were not proposing to miss it.

Everyone – including war workers – was supposed to take shelter when raiders were spotted and the sirens sounded. Sometimes a single German airplane would fly over, aiming to disrupt war factories and daily life as much as possible. To counteract this, raid spotters, usually factory staff, would be stationed on the roofs of factories, to raise the alarm if the raiders were closing in. Muriel Simkin worked in a munitions factory in Dagenham, Essex:

> We had to wait until the second alarm before we were allowed to go to the shelter. The first bell was a warning they were coming. The second was when they were overhead. They (the factory owners) did not want any time wasted. The planes might have gone straight past and the factory would have stopped for nothing …
>
> Sometimes the Germans would drop their bombs before the second bell went. On one occasion a bomb hit the factory before we were given permission to go to the shelter. The paint department went up. I saw several people flying through the air and I just ran home. I was suffering from shock and was worried about whether my own house had been hit. I was suspended for six weeks without pay. They would have been saved if they had been allowed to go after the first alarm. It was a terrible job but we had no option. We all had to do war work. We were risking our lives in the same way as the soldiers were.

5

SECOND PHASE

On 17 September 1940 Hitler postponed his plans for the invasion of Britain.

Despite this, the first phase of the Blitz continued for a total of fifty-seven nights from September until November 1940. During November 1940, bombers came every night bar one, when bad weather prevented flying.

Germany had four objectives in continuing the bombing:

- to demoralise the population so that Britain would seek peace with Germany.
- to disrupt war production in the capital.
- to tie down significant British military resources to deal with the bombing, and
- to show Stalin, the Russian leader, that Hitler's continuing aim was the defeat of Britain. In December 1940, however, long before the end of the Blitz, Hitler began planning the invasion of Russia.

Major war industries, such as aircraft engine production, were based in Manchester, making it a prime target for the Luftwaffe. It was bombed throughout the war, from August 1940 until Christmas 1944. This picture shows firefighters during a raid on the night of 7 December 1940; the heaviest bombing raids on the city occurred just over two weeks later, on the nights of 22 and 23 December. *Courtesy of the Imperial War Museum*

After 14 November, raids spread to other major cities and industrial centres across Britain, giving London some respite from the nightly attacks. This became known as the second phase of the Blitz, from November to February 1941.

One such target, Coventry, had experienced several small raids during July and August 1940, but on 14 November hundreds of bombers working in waves dropped incendiaries, high-explosive bombs and oil bombs through the night. Dr R. V. Jones, who was in charge of British scientific intelligence, later said that a miscalculation meant the German navigational equipment was not jammed as it should have been. As a result, the first wave of bombers ('pathfinders') were able to drop their bombs and light accurately the way for subsequent waves to continue the attack. Margaret Chifney was a member of the Women's Land Army. She spent one of her days off visiting Coventry and, in November 1940, decided to spend a second day's leave there:

My second visit I made with the other land girls and some soldiers from a local unit to a dance in the YMCA. We went in an army lorry.

After about an hour the air raid warning went but no-one seemed to be worried; we were told they don't come this far, 'they' being German planes. The next few minutes had the man eating his words for tonight they had got this far and came in force and to stay.

I had not seen any bombing in London. My five brothers were in the forces and my sister was in an aircraft factory and my father was making blackout blinds and curtains. My father and sister told me of the bombing for they were the only two of the family left in London, and until tonight I had not realised what they had been going through.

The warden was trying to get us all out of the building which was well alight by now but when we got outside every building seemed to be on fire and in the distance the flames were lighting up the cathedral. I was petrified and couldn't move, a warden dragged me to the ground as the scream of another bomb came but he left me to run to a woman who was on fire, he rolled her on the ground to put out the flames and took her to a shelter. I looked around to see if I could see any of the girls I had come with but more bombs were falling and I needed somewhere to shelter. The moon was like a huge torchlight and the roads had ice on them, the trees were sparkling with the frost. I heard another screaming bomb and threw myself behind a hedge and a short wall and covered my ears against the bang. I don't know how long I stayed, it seemed like hours, there were so many buildings burning now the firemen were helping people rather than trying to put the fires out, it was impossible. I knew that if I didn't move soon I would die of cold, how I wished I had my old breeches and boots on instead of a dress and these silly shoes, how could I run in these?

I tried to get an idea which way the station was. I thought if I got there I may be able to get back to base, so I got up and started to walk and then run a little in the direction of the railway, when I looked up and in the bright moonlight I saw a parachute with what looked like a dustbin on it so I found another wall to hide behind.

[This was a German parachute mine, originally a magnetic sea mine. When Allied Forces found a way to neutralise their effects at sea, German arms manufacturers redesigned the fuse and dropped the mine on a parachute, as a large bomb.]

I lay there, covered my ears and waited but the explosion did not come so I had another try for the station. I went up the wrong road twice and found myself almost back in the town when I recognised a black building that I knew was on the way to the station.

After what seemed like hours I saw the railway bridge and I thought 'at last' and then for the second time that night I was dragged to the ground, this time by a fireman. He said something and pointed to the railway bridge and hanging there like a chandelier was the land mine, the parachute caught on the bridge.

I spent the rest of the night wet, cold and very frightened, in a lady's coal cellar under her house. There were several other occupants. One poor lady had completely lost her mind; she was screaming and trying to get out saying her son was in the city – it was unbelievable.

How I got back is still a mystery. I had a ride in a car, a tractor, and the last transport I remember was a horse and cart but the welcome I got when I did arrive helped me to recover. I was so happy to see they were all safe, they thought I had been trapped in the building. I just collapsed in a heap and cried myself to sleep.

When I see people in films or on television falling out of windows with their clothes on fire I wonder how many people like me remember that it really did happen. It will stay with me forever.

When I returned to Coventry two weeks later to go home on leave there was nothing I could recognise, even the cathedral had only half one spire left – it was heartbreaking. I am pleased that the new cathedral has included some of the ruins – this way no one will ever forget so many heroes, police, wardens, firemen and most people who were not burnt themselves helped those who were burnt. It amazes me that anyone came out of there alive.

H.R. Clothier had started a new job as head of the Invoice Certification Department of Daimler Aero Engines as the war broke out and had moved to Coventry. He wrote:

The sirens went and all hell was let loose. The next day at work a colleague at work suggested Lilian [Mr Clothier's wife] and I stay at his place at Narborough in Leicester. So Lilian and I got ready when I got home and got to the town square and waited for the Leicester bus. Then the sirens went and we were well down the queue. Was I frightened? I'd got nerves like steel – steel that's long since had metal fatigue. My heart was in my boots. I must say about Lilian – she kept calm. The night before, when we went down to the shelter, everyone was quaking and she just sat on the steps knitting. Now I look back, her steady calm must have calmed the other inmates. Anyway we slowly moved up the queue, amid the sound of droning aeroplanes and then I saw the bus was full. Oh dear! But he was a tolerant bus conductor and let us get on. God I was relieved when the bus drove away. Narborough was a haven – I really thanked my colleague – not a sound all night.

In late 1940, Claire Lowry applied to join the Women's Royal Naval Service (WRNS). She went to their Portsmouth offices the morning after another night's bombing:

People were streaming out of Portsmouth, with cases, bundles, prams and bicycles – all carrying as many belongings as they could muster. The reason was clear – the devastation was terrible – terraces of houses, pubs, shops, all in smoking ruins.

The people had no homes anymore, so they were on their way to the country, no doubt village halls, cottages, would take them in and the WVS would provide food and comfort as they always did in those times. Meanwhile, I had to pick my way through the rubble along Hampshire Terrace and the police stopped me, saying it was too dangerous to go further.

As my Grandmother was terrified of the air raids, my Auntie and Uncle would stay with her overnight. There was an air raid shelter at the end of the road, so when the raid was on, they would rush to the shelter, whilst Uncle would rush to his bank to fire-watch. Grandmother could not walk very fast, so eventually they stayed in her house whenever a raid was on. One night they were in the back of the house when a bomb was dropped on a house nearby. Auntie thought that the roof had been blown off their house, so they tried to open the front door, but it was jammed, so they struggled in the dark to the front room to get out of the window, but Grandmother said, 'Look, the whole of the front is blown out', so they calmly walked out through the blown out window. Hurriedly, hustling grandmother along the avenue, Auntie went back to her flat in London Road, and they sat and recovered from the shock, until Uncle rejoined them. The next day, Auntie returned to the shattered house, to ascertain the damage. In the daylight, she saw that the whole front of Grandmother's house was devastated, but when Auntie carefully walked through the debris into the front room of the house, an amazing sight met her eyes. The glass blown from the large bay windows had splintered into hundreds of pieces, and they were firmly embedded into the walls of the room. In the sunlight the glass flashed like chandeliers, and tinkled like Chinese chimes.

The house was unliveable, so Grandmother, Uncle and Auntie went to Lovedean to live, until the repairs were made.

Manchester was another city in which major war industries were based. The first attacks were fairly light, but over Christmas 1940 the city was heavily bombed in raids noted by J. Grenville Atherton in his diary. His father was in charge of the works engineering department at Metropolitan Vickers, which built Lancaster bombers and which he refers to as 'Metrovickers':

Sunday, 22 December 1940 4th in Advent. Shortest Day: The 'raiders passed' went at 3.45 am. Got up at 8 am. Sirens went again 10.30 am so went for ride round Flixton. Roads quiet. Tyre punctured in back wheel as I got home.

Took liqueur glasses to Auntie Jessie for Christmas present. After tea called at Bernard's. At 6.40 pm sirens went followed by terrific gunfire. Went in their shelter with his two sisters and brother Ian.

Stayed till 10.00 pm then went home.

Fires burning over the dock area. Trafford Park factories on fire. All sky lit orange, red, pink. All quiet between guns. Dead silent … Always this stillness and silence. No 'in-between noises' unless a bomb lands near.

Heard ambulance/fire bell in distance.

Ran to Sevenways [a road junction] and went in the shelter; nobody in. A special constable poked his head in. Told me to stay. Ignored him because I knew my parents worried about me. Ran out. Just then more bombs landed on nearby industrial complex of T[rafford] Park; it sent along a cold breeze. Blast. Still not a soul in sight. Windows of houses reflect bright pink glow, pavements pink. Pink sunshine at night – eerie but interesting.

Ran up driveway of first house and pinched their metal dustbin lid, held it over my head against raining shrapnel and scooted home to family. No neighbours in our shelter for a change. Thankful to be home safe. All OK. Planes overhead continuously. Searchlight beams in field at back bounced off dirty low clouds and smoke. Bombs and gunfire all mixed up, can't tell which is which.

Commenting some years later and quoting further from his diary, he added:

We had been in the shelter since 10.30 last night (Sunday). The guns opened fire again and again, the noise was ear splitting. The 14-inch wall of our surface shelter, though reinforced with steel, shook many times. Mum looked pale and fretted about people being killed. She had dealt with hundreds of front line casualties having spent a short time in France in 1914 in the Voluntary

Aid Detachment of the Red Cross and four years at Elm
Bank war emergency hospital in Eccles until 1918, but
she said this is a different war …

Dad looked serious. He seemed very calm outwardly,
but uneasy. My sister was tired out and went to sleep. I, as
usual, became restless and fidgety and wanted to go out
to have a look. I felt better when I could see what was
going on instead of letting my imagination run riot.

A fairly bright orange and greenish light of burning
warehouses and chemicals blanketed the whole of the
north. Stretford, Old Trafford and the densely populated streets of Hulme seemed to be receiving the worst
of it, as was confirmed later. Fires could easily be seen
flaring over the centre of Manchester, and occasional
bright flashes showed up against the night sky as more
flammable material took hold. Canisters of small magnesium incendiary bombs fell everywhere. They were
nasty little things. All right for fireworks but not when
they were aimed at your head. Later on they carried
a small explosive charge to deter you from coming
too close.

Outside most houses for emergency use were a bucket
of sand or water, a stirrup pump and its 30ft of hosepipe.
In addition we kept our bath full of cold water.

One o'clock, two o'clock, three o'clock, four, five
and six o'clock, it went on. Our eyes smarted with the
smoke accompanied by a strong smell of cordite not
unlike our school chemy lab. Near Cowburn's down the
road in Trafford Park were open railway wagonloads of
sulphur as used for woollen bleaching amongst other
things. It was evil, poisonous stuff when it caught fire or
just smouldered …

A three-person stirrup pump team at work; one to direct the hose, one
to pump and one to keep the bucket topped up. Behind them is a brick
surface shelter, used where Anderson shelters were impractical.

Read 'Everybody's,' [a popular magazine] and nodded off. Heard shrapnel hit tiles and rattle into the gutters. This is definitely the worst raid we have had. Dozing and waking. Bomb hit electricity distribution kiosk round corner on Urmston Lane and put out elec. stove and lamp. Lit candles in jam jars.

All clear at 6.16 am. It has been 11 hours 36 minutes.

For good measure we had a short alarm at 6.45 am. You can imagine our mixed feelings – but all clear 45 mins later. Our little pet budgie was dead, all windows in glass vestibule at the side of the house broken and garage doors blown off. Sticky tape on windows not much good.

Monday 23rd December 1940

Father went to work without any sleep. He was quite unflappable. I am quite sure having a routine job to get on with, even if it is just doing the housework, helps you to keep going.

He said what we all need is time. Time to go to work. Time to put up with the raids. Time to catch up on sleep.

His department was responsible for the entire running of the hundreds of acres of factory and goodness knew what damage he was going to find.

My sister and I went to bed for an hour or two then got up and swept away broken glass and plaster. It was everywhere, in the carpet, curtains, even stuck in the soap and needless to say I cut my finger. Having no electricity was a nuisance. I bought a new cycle tyre for 7/4*d* (6/1d plus purchase tax 1/3d). Eddie and I went for a short ride round the district. Saw lots of bomb craters. Many new houses badly damaged in Humphrey Park Estate a mile away. Half of one avenue destroyed – 11 houses missing. Some killed. My friend Eddie and I felt guilty and intrusive and rode away.

In Trafford Park dozens of warehouses and factories damaged and still smoking. Rosser's timber yard on fire. All that lovely wood still blazing. They must have drained the Bridgewater Canal and Manchester Ship Canal nearly dry, or so it seemed.

A flour miller's was on fire – thousands of tons of it. Firemen were covered in sticky dough from the hose water. We had a good laugh, not at them, but with them, though there were tears in their laughter due to exhaustion. Two firemen lay on the ground with burnt hands, their faces white with flour, eyes red rimmed, like crumpled clowns ...

Smoke and dust seemed to be blowing in the cold wind from all directions. Came home via MetroVickers, which had been hit, but I could see my father's office window from Westinghouse Road and his office block looked unharmed. A water main had been torn up within the factory and firemen were pumping it away.

Luckily few people were injured because they had a spotting system to warn if raiders approached near, and because yesterday was a Sunday there were not as many as usual on the night shift and most of the offices were empty. There were about 1,000 firemen including auxiliaries, and several shelters to take many workers and staff, probably several thousand.

The main 'tunnel' shelter underneath the main 'aisles' or machine shops would withstand anything but a direct hit. It had an operating theatre and full time medical staff and fifty beds for casualties ...

Families went back to their houses to collect bedding
and blankets and warm clothing. There was insufficient
organisation for the salvaging and reclamation of clothes
and property. If they could not find their own home they
just took anything suitable that was lying about. Most
houses were just a shell, with bricks and floorboards
spilled out in a sloping heap on to the cobbled streets.
There was no space for ambulances to drive. Also no
room for Anderson shelters in many cases because there
were no gardens, although some had put them in the
back yard. Consequently more were killed and crushed
and burned.

The bombers were back the following night:

Father came home from work tired out. He said that
two landmines (parachute bombs) had caused fearfully
expensive damage and he was in the process of setting
up a programme of repair work which was the main
task of his department, Works Engineering, and in addition carried the full responsibility for all ARP services
throughout the massive plant.

After tea we continued to tidy the house, carrying on
as normal, when the sirens sounded their wavy 'up and
down' howling. Fires were still alight in the darkness so
no doubt Jerry easily found his direction …

My sister had spent the night with friends in Sale,
not far away, and they came back with her in the morning to see if we were safe. Apart from the usual cracked
plaster and most of the leaded-lights being broken, we
were thankful for no injuries. Nearly every house in
Melville Road was destroyed by a land mine. There were

several casualties. Albert's wife lost her arm. To save his life, firemen had to chop off a young lad's foot with an axe because he was trapped in a collapsing building. They both recovered. The girls' high school where my sister attended received a direct hit, a merciful blessing the girls were on holiday for Christmas. Uncle Fred's house in Ravenswood Road next to the school lost its roof. Uncle Tom's house was ripped open while they were sheltering. Metrovickers was hit again and the main turbine and generator workshops damaged badly.

The centre of Manchester was on fire, water mains broken, and offices and banks and warehouses adjacent to Mosley Street and Piccadilly were blazing fiercely. The commercial centre of the city came off worse than factories and mills in the northern suburbs. A large part of the historic Free Trade Hall, home of the Halle orchestra, was destroyed by fire.

Nearer home a small HE bomb went off in Mr Dakin's (our headmaster) front garden in Urmston Lane round the corner and in Arlington Road two houses only eight doors away got a direct hit.

After helping his mother nail weatherproof sheeting to the window frames, Grenville Atherton set off to the safety of his aunt's house outside the city:

Main roads into Manchester were impassable due to debris and collapsed buildings, smouldering fires, telegraph poles uprooted, smashed furniture, vehicles and police barriers and bomb craters and so on. Burst water mains and sewage had formed deep puddles. Being Christmas Eve few services were available.

I got off the bus half a mile from the city centre, carrying my little 'evacuation' suitcase over concrete blocks, fallen walls and steel girders twisted with heat. Danger notices pointed out deep basements that were not easily recognised. The main shopping centres, Deansgate and Market Street, were smashed to bits, a chaotic litter. Buildings were knocked down and shops and offices open to the cold grey sky for everyone to see, still crumbling and cracking. Ladies and menswear, bedding, household goods, furniture, books, foodstuffs were scattered in confusion. Anybody could pick it up and probably did. The wind was just blowing it all to waste.

There must have been bodies under all that mess yet many were saved because the first night of the blitz was a Sunday when the town was relatively empty. There were others like me carrying some luggage out of the city. I called to a man, and he replied that Piccadilly bus station 'had gone' but that buses were going north from Fairfield Street. Otherwise it was strangely and unexpectedly quiet. No crowds of sightseers. No heavy demolition gangs. I saw firemen, wardens and police and rescue workers climbing in and out of the delicately balanced shells of buildings which looked as if they would crumble like a biscuit at a touch, looking and listening for any trapped victims.

Eventually he arrived at a hotel and met his relatives:

Christmas Day
My father telephoned from work to wish us a happy Christmas under the circumstances. He and mother were all right. We ate a lovely Christmas dinner with 8 other guests present. Afterwards some of us went for a walk

round the village. It was fine and cold with a blue sky. No air raids to worry us.

The parish church had a decorated tree next to the bell tower. That evening my aunt (the welfare officer) attended a special service to pray for the victims of air raids everywhere.

Boxing Day

Today we all transferred to the Hanging Gate Hotel across the moors on the Huddersfield road to a village called Diggle. The landlord, appropriately named Mr. Moorhouse, was a big, fat individual, bald, with a lady I thought was his mother but was his wife. He said he was willing to take in any evacuees and homeless people from Manchester as long as they could pay, and the blitz was good for business and laughed his head off at his 'joke'. He seemed quite unconcerned.

Outside the hotel, which was beautifully furnished and appointed, was a hand painted sign: 'This gate hangs well and hinders none. Refresh and pay, and carry on.' We could pay. But what if we could not?

… On Friday the newspapers were published, which said a north west town had been attacked. It was rather non-committal due to censorship until the Germans admitted they had bombed Manchester. It was stated in the paper that much needless suffering had been caused to survivors because some emergency services had been on holiday. This same day Auntie Mollie, and Barbara and Joan (they were a couple of years older than I) went by bus on a very cold day to Salford and Stretford town halls, respectively, to try to arrange urgent repairs to their home in Salford and Uncle Fred's in Stretford. They were told not to be impatient and that they were not the only ones with a problem and if they could afford to spend time at a hotel they were obviously not desperate for help. They had lost all their ration books and identity cards and insurance policies. They were so upset at the callous attitude they were in tears. Both uncles had served throughout the First World War and they managed to get some satisfaction the following week. My other aunt had a lingerie shop on Regent Road, Salford, which had its windows smashed and she had no problem at all with the town hall officials. All our homes were eventually repaired by local tradespeople after submitting claims to the assessors who came round to inspect the damage on behalf of the War Damage Commission. The money was either paid to you or to the contractor who carried out the repairs.

Experience showed the importance of spotting incendiary bombs quickly, before they caused major fires. As with many other areas of ARP, the initial response to the call for volunteers was patchy. The Fire Watchers Order, introduced in September 1940, compelled owners of businesses to ensure that someone on the premises was responsible for fire-watching at all times. Further legislation in October 1940 gave ARP wardens and others the power to enter premises to prevent fires from spreading.

On 29 December 1940, incendiary bombs caused massive fires across the city of London. William Sansom wrote that:

Christmas in London that year was quiet. The day after Boxing Day a light raid; but two nights later – on the

29th – there occurred a very heavy fire raid which burnt out so large an area of the City of London, and which extended over other parts of London including Westminster. The sirens sounded early – as usual on those long winter nights – and the raid developed in force.

In his book, *The Forgotten Front line*, Barry Hollis wrote:

By 6.15 pm [German bombers] were dropping the first sticks of bombs and incendiaries of a savage attack, concentrated on a half-mile square section of the City of London to the north of St Pauls. Packed into this area were countless old buildings, many of them built of wood, tucked into a maze of courts, alleyways, and lanes each so narrow that it was impossible to get a motor appliance or wheeled escape into them. To get to fires within this warren of offices, warehouses, and small businesses, hoses had to be run from the nearest street or pumps manhandled off units and trailers onto small barrow like wheels and then pushed and shoved to where they were needed.

The Germans had chosen the day well. The river had one of its lowest tides with yards of mudflats stretching from the banks towards the narrow stream in the middle of the tideway. Being the Sunday after Christmas there were no office workers to be found and many of those who did live there, such as caretakers, were away with friends. Consequently only a few people were in the area and of this few only a conscientious minority went onto the rooftops to firewatch when the alert sounded. Most of the buildings were double padlocked and firemen and ARP personnel were severely hampered and delayed in getting to the flaring incendiaries.

Reginald Bell was Group Co-ordinating Officer of the London Civil Defence Region:

> At 6.30 pm the attack began. Basket after basket of incendiaries clattered on the roofs and streets of the City of London. All round St Paul's Cathedral fires sprang up and spread. Fire bombs fell on the cathedral roof but by the devoted activity of watchers who knew every nook and cranny of the terrain all were cast off and the Cathedral was saved.
>
> Other firewatchers, with equal diligence and success, extinguished every incendiary bomb which fell on the Guildhall. Alas their efforts were in vain. Thousands of bombs on unattended or inaccessible roofs all round started fires which roared like furnaces in the high wind. Embers and incandescent particles varying in size from half a crown to a saucer swirled into the air and swept like a sparkling snowstorm through the streets and among the chimney-tops, laying a blanket of glowing brands upon roofs and gables …

Aylmer Firebrace takes up the story:

> About 7 p.m. on this fateful night things started to warm up, so, accompanied by Mr. A. P. L. Sullivan, my senior staff officer, I started off on a tour of the fires. In Southwark serious fires were developing, and in Queen Victoria Street the situation looked ugly. London Bridge Railway Station, together with the buildings in the Station Approach, was well alight, whilst opposite Guy's Hospital an uncontrolled fire was in progress.

Large falls of I.B.s [Incendiary Bombs] had everywhere occurred, and the German claim that during this night they dropped some 100,000 incendiaries may well be true. Everywhere fires were developing. Fire watchers and fire parties were conspicuous by their absence – it was the weekend! There was the inevitable shortage of water; three thirty-six inch and twelve other large mains, as well as the dirty-water main, were damaged; to increase the danger of the situation the tide was out when the water was most needed, making it difficult either for fire boats or land machines to obtain a supply from the river.

By 8 p.m. some three hundred pumps were at work in and around the City; the resources of the Region were to be seriously strained before all fires were in hand, let alone extinguished. Bombers could be heard overhead – fresh waves kept arriving. More and more fires were joining up and turning into conflagrations. The situation was rapidly deteriorating and no one could possibly foretell where the fires would eventually stop or be stopped.

Before long Mr. Sullivan and I abandoned our car, for the streets, piled high with debris, were impassable to wheeled traffic. From Cannon Street we proceeded on foot to Redcross Street Fire Station, which lies to the north-east of St. Paul's.

One by one telephone lines fail; the heat from the fires penetrates to the control room and the atmosphere is stifling. Earlier in the evening, after a bomb falls near, the station lights fail – a few unshaded electric hand lamps now supply bright pin-point lights in sharp contrast to a few oil lamps and some perspiring candles. The firewomen on duty show no sign of alarm, though they must know, from the messages passing, as well as from the anxious tones of officers, that the situation is approaching the desperate. Suddenly the door of the control room is thrown open and a Civil Defence warden, his face black and perspiring, his eyes bloodshot and inflamed, shouts: 'Your bloody roof's alight!' He doesn't wait for an answer and probably never hears the undismayed, if undisciplined, cry of 'Whoopee!' [from a firewoman] to be suitably echoed by the remainder.

A woman fire officer arrives; she has been forced to evacuate the sub-station to which she was attached, the heat having caused its asphalt yard to burst into flames. Instead of moving to safety, she has probed her way farther into the danger area. It is quite obvious that it cannot now be long before Redcross Street Fire Station, nearly surrounded by fire, will have to be abandoned. Mr. Sullivan and I make our way into the street.

The high wind which accompanies conflagrations is now stronger than ever, and the air is filled with a fierce driving rain of red-hot sparks and burning brands. The clouds overhead are a rose-pink from the reflected glow of the fires, and fortunately it is light enough to pick our way eastward down Fore Street. Here fires are blazing on both sides of the road; burnt-out and abandoned fire appliances lie smouldering in the roadway, their rubber tyres completely melted. The rubble from collapsed buildings lying three and four feet deep, makes progress difficult in the extreme. Scrambling and jumping, we use the bigger bits of fallen masonry as stepping stones, and eventually reach the outskirts of the stricken area.

A few minutes later L.F.B. officers wisely evacuate Redcross Street Fire Station, and now the only way to escape for the staff and for the few pumps' crews remaining in the area lies through Whitecross Street. Firemen and firewomen, making their way between St. Giles Church, Cripplegate, on their right, and a warehouse on their left, both ablaze, descend into an air-raid shelter, from where they drop on to the Metropolitan Railway line, finally to emerge at Smithfield Goods Depot.

The City of London was beginning to resemble a scene from Dante's *Inferno* as William Sansom wrote:

The miracle occurred at some time past eleven. The all-clear sounded. The fires were then rising to a fury – it was a windy night – and in the City of London the wind-spread of fire was on a gigantic scale. However, by some dispensation of the weather on German airfields the bombers never returned with the weight of explosives that would have aggravated so successfully an already disastrous situation. In Westminster the position was not grave – though there was trouble indeed and of course a scarcity of fire-fighting appliances, for most had been drawn on force towards the City of London. Of particular incidents, the LCC Ambulance Station in Regency Street was wrecked, and one of the war's largest craters opened outside the Egyptian Embassy – a vast hole measuring 42 feet across. Perhaps the greatest communal danger to the City was the fire at City Hall, in rooms just above the Report Centre itself. An oil bomb set fire to the Council Chamber on the first floor. The room became a mass of flames. Those on the spot ran their internal hoses straight to the fire – but there was no water, explosives outside had broken the vital mains. All that the fire-staff could do was to limit the spread of small fires in other rooms: meanwhile the main fire burnt on, one floor above the room controlling the whole of the City's defences. The official Fire Services arrived, but were faced with the same difficulty of obtaining water. Altogether this fire burnt for some four hours before it was thoroughly controlled – and throughout its quenching much water poured down the stairs and into the basement. The low level of the basement was knee-deep in water – but fortunately the control room itself was raised a few steps higher. Interruption was caused to a main switchboard – though the important direct lines were not affected. These the control room staff kept operating throughout the period of the fire, when perhaps at any moment the blaze might have suddenly blossomed, as fires do, and brought the ceilings and floors above crashing down into the vital room beneath.

Although London had been spared further damage, it had suffered badly. Reginald Bell:

The water supply of London failed, important mains being shattered by High Explosive bombs … only by dragging heavy suction-pipes across the mud from the fireboats in mid-stream could water be brought to the bank. In the river-bed, hour by hour, firemen toiled in the eerie glare from a wall of fire, heaving, straining and coaxing slimy pipes and slippery couplings into a battery of lines for vital water supply.

… two [fire]officers and fourteen men were killed and 250 officers and men injured in fighting the fifteen hundred fires that blazed in London that night.

As the tide turned the fires were brought under control. The real damage had been done in the first five hours of the attack but daylight showed the extent of the damage:

Mountains of calcined stone lay in the streets; forests of twisted girders sprouted ... from red-hot basements which glowed sullenly for days.

Millions of gallons of water poured uselessly away from fractured mains so deep under heaps of rubble that turncocks and water officers were faced with hopeless problems. In provision shops roast carcasses, fowls and foodstuffs filled the air with strange, mixed odours.

Aylmer Firebrace summed up the night, and the lessons learned from it:

The Regional record for the night showed six confla-grations needing more than one hundred pumps apiece, twenty-eight fires each needing over thirty pumps, fifty-one fires at about the twenty-pump mark, 101 requiring up to ten pumps apiece, and 1,286 fires which had to make do with one pump each. The great majority of these fires were inside the L.C.C. area. Just under 2,000 pumps from the London Region were at work, whilst 300 were sent in to London from surrounding regions. Before the war there were only 1,850 pumps protecting the whole of Great Britain.

This raid showed:

1. The urgent necessity to provide open water, either by flooding the basement of demolished buildings, or as best suited the locality.
2. The necessity for occupiers of every building to fur-nish their own first line of fire defence, by arranging for

   a portion of their staff to sleep on the premises every
   night, and for it to be a point of honour for owners and
   employees not to allow their building to burn.
3. The need for fire brigades to develop a special section which would produce water for fire-fighting, no
   matter what the conditions.

This raid became known as the Second Great Fire of
London. The damage caused by incendiaries was a particular concern. Pre-war, the planners' main concern had been
protecting against poison gas. Early raids shifted the focus
to high-explosive bombs, but later raids, especially the
raids on Coventry and the City of London, showed that
the small 1kg electron incendiary, dropped in thousands,
could raze large areas, overwhelming the fire brigades and
ARP workers.

The Government responded quickly. On 31 December
1940, Herbert Morrison, the Minister for Home Security,
broadcast on the radio that 'Britain shall not burn' and
announced that the Government intended to introduce
compulsory fire-watching. Every building – occupied or
unoccupied – would have to have its fire watcher.

The *Western Daily Press* reported him saying; 'I must say
this plainly to each one of you. It is your duty to yourself, to
your neighbours and friends, to your city and your country to guard your own homes, business or factory from fire
bombs. You cannot stop high explosive bomb from burst-
ing, but you can stop a fire bomb from starting a fire.' He
concluded with the cry: 'Fall in, the fire-bomb fighters.'

Rose Uttin, aged 41 when she started writing her
diary, was a member of a fire party. She lived in Wembley,
Middlesex, with her husband Bill, mother, and daughter

Dora, who was aged 13 when the war broke out. Bill was also a member of the fire-watching party at home and in his workplace at the Royal Exchange in London:

20th January 1941
11.30 pm and no alert so we are off to bed. Still downstairs in the lounge of course – I wonder how long it will be before we can safely sleep upstairs again.

At 4 am we were awakened by persistent knocking at the front door. I thought at first something had happened to mother but it was the firewatcher. He had made a mistake and he didn't know how to contact the next couple. He sounded so tired but said he could not go home until he found them – rather like Mary and her lamb; it has not stopped raining since 4 o'clock yesterday so expect the shelter is full of water. Something will have to be done about it – an added base of concrete Bill thinks.

22nd Jan
We had this evening at 7.30 am our second meeting and we gained 21 new 'watchers' – now it is hoped that it will mean one night on duty in 9 instead of the 6 as first planned. It is imperative we keep awake for the sirens are not penetrating enough when one is sound asleep. This war has made us meet our neighbours and chat with them – and most of them seem eager to help. I hope the enthusiasm will be kept up …

I looked in at the shelter today, rain water has seeped in and it is now on a level with the top of the steps – we shall need a boat if we are to use it.

Jan 30th

The Dene firewatchers cannot get enough volunteers so they have to do 4 to 6 hours per night on patrol – good thing when conscription comes in for some of them … I phoned Laurie C and she still has the little baby to mind.

They had a land mine at the end of the road Xmas week and another bomb in their garden so are without windows back and front and 2 ceilings down … Next Wednesday we are on from 2 till 4 am, the worst watch of all as sleep is out of the question. Bill has been asked to stay at the (Royal) Exchange on Monday and firewatch there. They are a group of 10 – and 3 paid watchers – an unlucky number I wonder?

Feb 2nd 1941

Today we had firefighting practice on the green in Rosslyn Crescent. I manned the pump and demonstrated with the hose – putting out the bomb and the fire on the supposed curtains. It is not as easy to use as one would expect – but I managed it. We hope to have another one soon with real furniture to burn.

4th Feb 1941

Tonight is our first watch with the alert which went at 7 pm – we have had occasional bursts of gunfire and one or two 'rats' passed over but did not drop anything. The first quarter of the moon is up and it is icy again underfoot – I do hope nothing happens for most people around have not taken their pails in and of course the water is frozen. This afternoon I brought the sandbags in and stood them in front of the fire for they were solid – they must be loose before we can use them. I have a helmet (tin) in front of me as I write, the inside is like those used as crash helmets by the speedway riders.

Feb 14th
The shelter is full of water. We really must get it empty for insects are beginning to get in there and it will not be healthy for too long. The all clear went at 11 pm.

Local brigades could not cope with the huge fires alone. They were lacking in equipment and people, and in organisation. Co-operation between brigades was difficult with over one thousand local brigades, individually organised and administered, using local uniforms, drills and equipment. The Home Office could only advise, and was often ignored. Some pumps and their crews sent to reinforce London in December had had to stand by uselessly as differences in connectors meant they could not couple with fire hydrants or water carriers. In April 1941, a group led by Herbert Morrison set out the principles of a unified National Fire Service (NFS), although for security reasons no announcement was made until 14 September. At its height in late 1942/early 1943, there would be 350,000 members of the NFS.

At the same time, the problem of water supplies began to be dealt with by forming 'static water tanks'. The basements of thousands of bombed buildings were made water tight, filled with water and marked with the letters EWS – emergency water supply. Prefabricated steel water tanks were erected on bombsites.

Individually, incendiaries could usually be easily dealt with by using a stirrup pump or covering with sand or earth in the first few minutes. The problems began when, left to burn, they started a bigger fire. On 6 August 1941 the Ministry of Home Security announced the formation of the 'Fire Guard', to be led by the MP Ellen Wilkinson. This was fundamentally a reorganisation of the existing fire watchers and fire parties, to be organised and trained locally by ARP services. The aim of the Fire Guard was to spot incendiaries as quickly as possible, put them out or call the NFS if the fire looked like it was getting out of control.

Members of the Fire Guard were organised into stirrup pump teams, each comprising three people and working on rotas. In towns and cities the aim was to have seven stirrup pump teams to every thirty houses or 150 yards (140m).

One month later enrolment in the Fire Guard became compulsory for men not already doing defence work, followed, in August 1942, by an order under which women aged between 20 and 45, and men between 18 and 60, had to register if they had not already done so.

Tom Mogg recalled fighting incendiaries as a young boy, at Plumstead Baths in London, where his father ran the emergency mortuary:

At a later raid, a cluster of fire bombs hit the Baths; staff were busy putting some of them out, so I went upstairs to our flat to check we were all right. On looking through the kitchen window I could see a fire bomb sticking out of the second-class swimmer roof. I ran upstairs, out onto our roofs, collecting a bucket of sand to find another bomb alight on the flat roof over the second-class ladies' hot baths. I covered it with sand, but it burnt through the bucket – another did the trick, plus spraying it with water. Now I had to deal with the bomb

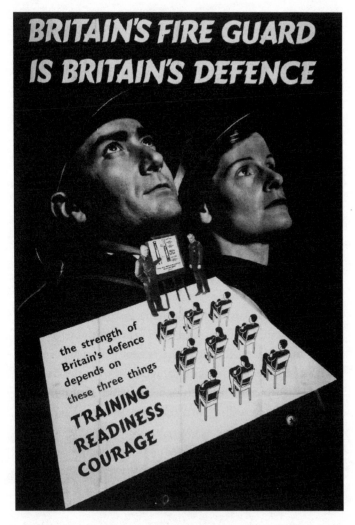

BRITAIN'S FIRE GUARD IS BRITAIN'S DEFENCE

the strength of
Britain's defence
depends on
these three things
TRAINING
READINESS
COURAGE

Incendiary bombs caused massive destruction and so, in 1941, the government created the Fire Guard. This expanded dramatically the volunteer street fire parties and firewatchers, and made fire-watching duties compulsory in towns and cities, beyond factories and other essential areas. This poster encouraged people to sign up for training. *Courtesy of The National Archives* in the swimmer roof; taking the last bucket of sand. I climbed out of our kitchen window onto the flat roof of the offices, then climbed on the swimmer roof and tried to run up it – but slid down again – after two attempts I kicked off my shoes and made it at the third. But this also needed at least two loads of sand which were outside our front door. When I reached to climb into our kitchen, Father was there so I asked him to get the sand. This seemed to do the trick, then I put on my shoes, and Father and I went down into the second-class pool hall. The pool was full, as an emergency water supply, but the roof was alight where the bomb had come through. Apart from a lantern there were no lights on. Father told me to run out the 3-inch fire hose; he would follow up untwisting the hose as he came, and I would run right round the pool using the dressing boxes as a guide (so that we would not run into each other in the dark). By the time I got to the fire hose wheel Father was ready with the hose. On it went, spraying all over the fire. At last Father told me to shut the hose off, but forgot which way he was standing and fell into the pool with an almighty splash. I felt my way in the dark to the side of the pool and called out in vain. He had become disoriented and was out in the middle of the pool somewhere. The only light came from our hand lantern and the flashes of gunfire seen through the broken glass in the roof lights, so I ran back to the entrance and switched on the main lights. Father could now see the side of the bath and climbed out. When we arrived back in the basement, there was one other casualty: one of the staff had kicked a fire bomb away from the building, and it had stuck to his shoe and burnt his foot.

NEW STRATEGIES

In early 1941, the Luftwaffe attacked ports in the west and south-west of England, and there were smaller raids elsewhere. Admiral Doenitz, head of the German Navy, wanted the Luftwaffe's support in the Battle of the Atlantic. Over the next few months the Germans targeted ports in every region of the UK: Bristol, Belfast, Newcastle, London, Sunderland and Swansea.

ARP warden Basil Radford was on fire-watching duty the first night of the Blitz on Swansea in 1941:

Feb 19
I was making a model of a Lysander plane when the sirens opened up at 7.38 pm. This was my night for fire-watching; we went out in pairs, my partner was Prof. B Farrington who lived opposite. I put on my heavy coat, it is very cold.

The Prof kept his side of the road and watched my side, particularly the roof and I did the same from my side.

The sound of the German planes was soon heard and flares were dropped, the whole crescent was lit up. What an eerie feeling it gave one, one felt so exposed. Within a minute the incendiary bombs began to fall. A large number came down in our small sector and lit up the scene still further, most of them fell in the roadway and gardens. I noticed one on a small tree which was soon alight. It seemed best to let them burn out since some might be explosive and dangerous to approach. Then the prof called out to me – 'there is one on your roof!' My heart sank into my boots. What could I do to prevent the house burning down? I went back into the house where my mother (aged 74), my sister and her young son lived. My sister and I went up to the top of the house to see if the bomb had come through – it had not. I then told my sister to get my mother and the boy across the road into the house of Mr Ireland who has a good cellar. Even this crossing of the road was dangerous as the HE bombs were coming down, but it seemed the lesser of two evils. By this time the stirrup pump had been brought into our hall … but it takes three to work a hand stirrup pump. I then went into the back garden to see if I could get a view of the bomb. At that moment two soldiers who were on leave jumped over the low garden wall and offered help. That made three of us, so the stirrup pump could be worked. We went up to the top of the house. It proved a difficult task, the bomb had not yet burnt through the ceiling. We tried to play a stream of water on it through the window. This was unsuccessful. Next we tried to throw a sandbag on it with no success. We had to wait until the bomb burnt through the ceiling; as soon as this happened it could be dealt with. The fire came through quickly in five minutes. The working of the stir-rup pump was a very arduous business, the water had to be carried up from the bathroom on the floor below. We kept our bath full of water every night for such an emergency and it proved invaluable, we were able to fill the buckets quickly. During all this time the HEs were coming down and we continually flattened out on the bedroom floor, though little good it would have been from a direct hit. We got the fire out.

Densely populated and with industries producing military vehicles, weapons, fighter planes and bombers, Birmingham was a prime target for the Luftwaffe between August 1940 and April 1943. It was, after London and Liverpool, the most heavily bombed city in the United Kingdom.

Don Thompson, born in 1927, lived with his mother and stepfather in Hall Green, a suburb of the city. The purpose of the raids, he was clear:

> was to terrify the population. The city centre was com-pletely destroyed and there was no military value at all ...
>
> Morale was quite strong. The ARP wardens would visit every house and make certain that people were all right and we used to go into each other's homes for a cup of tea. We were always very conscious of the loca-tion of people in houses so you did not sleep in the bedroom, but sleep down stairs so that you would not tumble through the floors if a bomb hit. So Mother and stepfather were in one room and I was in the back room downstairs. And if you went out you always told people so that the wardens would not waste time digging for you if something happened.

Born in America, William Joyce was brought up in Ireland and came to England in the 1930s, where he joined the British Union of Fascists. He went to Germany in 1939 and from there he broadcast weekly programmes to Britain on behalf of the German propaganda ministry, aimed at lowering the morale of the civilian population. Lord Haw-Haw was the name given in Britain to several broadcasters from the Nazi-run radio station Reichssender Hamburg, of whom Joyce was the best known. The nickname in Britain came about because the broadcasts always began 'Germany calling, Germany calling' in an upper-class tone.

British government requests that people should not listen had little effect but neither, for that matter, did Joyce's broadcasts.

Roy Clevely, aged 11 when war broke out, was living with his parents in the Redfield area of Bristol. The city was heavily bombed between November 1940 and April 1941:

I can always remember my father liked to try and tune into Haw-Haw crashing the BBC News. It could have been 9 o'clock or 10 o'clock – he was frowned upon a little bit for being pro-German but that was not the case, he was just interested in what Lord Haw-Haw, as he was called, had to say …

Haw-Haw's mother used to live in [the] Fishponds area of the city and he knew the city very well …

I remember him telling us 'the Luftwaffe would be visiting Bristol before very long' and naming all the streets – Castle Street, Mary le Port, Denmark Street, you name them he had them. And he said, 'Bristol you will be losing your famous …' whatever and lo and behold on the first blitz the very centre of Bristol was taken out, it was as accurate as that. We knew a great deal of it was false but when Bristol caught it, it was absolutely true. And later it came out that as early as 1936 they (German airmen) were flying over Bristol and other cities and photographing them.

As a young boy I castigated him with all the language I could think of. Morale stood up incredibly well because in times of danger I really feel that the human spirit tends to rally and coalesce and I feel that the citizens of Bristol – of course very divided politically, in all shades, really did come together and there was tremendous self-help and mutual help that occurred and it helped us to get through those dangerous times.

Of course we always listened to Churchill's speeches. I suppose we wanted to see both sides of the story. We knew that the German propaganda was just that – a great deal was false but when they went for Bristol it was spot on. [Churchill's speeches] were tremendously uplifting and the man gave us tremendous hope and we used to doubt him at times – another country has fallen, prisoners taken and so on. [But at the] time we had this tremendous faith and confidence in him and in the coalition government.

Across the country, crime continued to rise. At Leeds Assizes on 5 March 1941, Justice Charles said:

More than two whole days have been occupied in dealing with cases of looting which have occurred in one city (Sheffield). When a great city is attacked by bombs on a heavy scale, numbers of houses and their contents are left exposed and deprived of their natural defences. Necessarily these are the homes of comparatively poor people, since they are by far the most numerous.

In many cases these looters have operated on a wholesale scale. There were actually two men who had abandoned well-paid positions, one of them earning £7 (equivalent to £356 today) to £9 (£457) a week, and work of public importance, and who abandoned it to take up the obviously more remunerative occupation of looting. The task of guarding shattered houses from prowling thieves, especially during the blackout, is obviously beyond the capacity of any police force. In view of the fact and having regard to the cowardly, abominable nature of the crime the perpetrators of which are preying upon the property of poor folk rendered homeless and often killed, the Legislature has provided that those found guilty of looting from premises damaged or vacated by reason of attacks by the enemy are on conviction liable to suffer death or penal servitude for life. Thus the law puts looters into the category of murderers, and the day may well be approaching when they will be treated as such.

Clydebank has the unenviable title of the most bombed town in Scotland. On 13 March 1941, 236 bombers attacked. Most returned the following night.

Tryphena Nixon (née Hislop), a teenager and ambulance driver, lived in nearby Bearsden. She wrote:

It was after midnight when our first call came and we started up our vehicle and began the journey as ordered down to Anniesland and thence to Scotstoun and Clydebank, there to await further orders from police or air raid wardens ...

As we progressed slowly along Dumbarton Road, almost every window on either side was shattered and each house had its curtains billowing out from empty window frames like spectres in the night waving their arms helplessly before the fires which burned within.

These ghost-like arms seemed to cry to us as we passed, yet so few people were abroad – most of them tucked safely away (we hoped) in their air-raid shelters.

James Hastings, the deputy town clerk of Clydebank, shared the duties of ARP controller for the burgh with two other senior officials:

> I phoned into the control centre and was told that nothing out of the ordinary was happening and there was no need for me to come down to Clydebank. I had intended to go on to perhaps supper or something at the house of one of my friends who were with me and I left the telephone number of that house in the control centre so that they could contact me if necessary.
>
> I went on to this friend's house, no call came through, and I think it must have been the unusually long period of the barrage which made me begin to wonder if this was rather different from what I had experienced before. I seem to remember trying to get in touch with the control centre again, but not being able to.
>
> I could not find out what was happening because there was always a tremendous security clamp on any information about air raids unless from official sources, and I was speaking from a private telephone, and … deciding that it was perhaps time that I was getting home, and home to me at that time really meant the office because we were sleeping in the office most of the time.

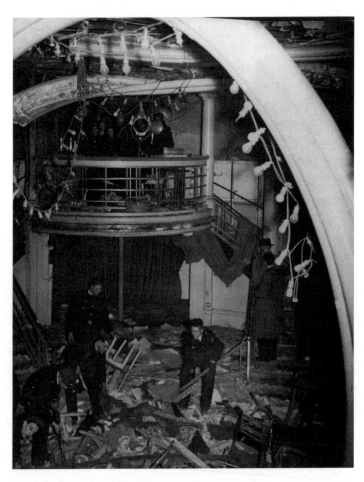

On 8 March 1941, the Café de Paris, a fashionable night club in London's Piccadilly, was devastated when a bomb fell through a ventilation shaft and exploded in the basement, killing more than thirty diners, staff, and members of the band, including band-leader 'Snakehips' Johnson. Survivors told of looters stealing jewellery, wallets and handbags from the dead and injured as they lay trapped in the rubble.

As Hastings walked towards Clydebank, he noted:

> There had been very little damage that I could see, proceeding along Dumbarton Road, but immediately I got to the Clydebank boundary the whole scene was one of devastation.

Arriving at the Control Centre, he realised very quickly that services were overwhelmed:

> Fires everywhere with fire engines and fire pumps standing by, many of them doing nothing because:
> 1.   Many of them were without petrol.
> 2.   The water main on Kilbowie Hill had been severed and all the mains in the lower part of the town served by the Kilbowie Road mains were without water and the fire hydrants were thus useless.
> 3.   The fire engines in the lower end of the town near to emergency water supply storage tanks near the canal had to use long runs of hoses, and the constant hauling of these among the tremendous piles of broken glass that littered the streets had punctured many of them until they were virtually useless.

Added to that, blocked roads prevented service crews from other districts from getting through.

> I decided to go to Bothwell Street in Glasgow to the office of the Petroleum Department, which I reached round about lunchtime.
> The office was virtually empty – only a young lad and a couple of typists. I showed him my credentials and

Rescue workers search through the rubble of Eglington Street in Belfast in
May 1941. News of the first major raids on the city on Easter Monday and
Tuesday was not widely broadcast. This raid was concentrated on the dock
area of the city. *Courtesy of the Imperial War Museum*

described the situation as vividly as I could, and asked if a load of petrol could be sent down immediately. He obviously had no authority and after a bit of bargaining I asked him to get in touch with someone in authority.

He did phone somebody and I've no doubt he did his best but the answer was that of all things I was to come back in the afternoon and ask for Mr So and So and he would no doubt be able to help me. This was merely another example of the sort of peacetime easy-going attitude that I had experienced from most of the government departments at the time.

I remember asking him to get this gentleman on the phone again and having a devilish barney over the phone but really I might as well have been talking to a stone wall.

In the event, I had the idea I might as well go down to the petrol company depot at Bowling but before I left Glasgow I remembered that I had heard of a petrol depot – somewhere in the Port Dundas area. I finally discovered it without much trouble, got hold of the manager, told him who I was, and what I wanted.

I've forgotten what the number of gallons was, but it was in hundreds of gallons and cans, a ridiculously high figure in those days of strict petrol rationing.

I'll never forget the difference in his attitude from that of the Petroleum Office people. He seemed at least to have heard that something had happened down at Clydebank because in five minutes I was out of the place with an assurance that there would be a lorry load of petrol down in Clydebank as soon as I would be there: and he was as good as his word.

I went straight back down and there was a lorry load of petrol in cans in half an hour or so thereafter; and we lost no time in getting it distributed among lorries, fire-engines, etc. that were non-operative because of petrol shortage. From then on, we had no trouble on that account.

Mary Haggerty was a child at the time living in the tenements of the town. The house across the road from her took a direct hit:

We realised we could not stay in the close, but where could we go? Round the back courts were stone shelters, but we always said we would never use them as they were only death traps, but it was all we had.

We went into one nearest our close, it was dark in the shelter, and we could hear the bombs falling. And I knew by the sound they were very near, and again one landed very close, there was a terrible bang and I swear our shelter went up in the air and down again – we never thought it could have done this and still stay in one piece.

It so happened that the shelter next to ours had been hit, and all the men had to go and try to get out the survivors from under the rubble, people had sheltered in the wash house and it was a mass of rubble, they were all killed …

We went up our stairs, the staircase windows were out and the doors had been blown off all the houses … I remember we just stood at our window, I mean the wide open space that used to be our windows, and watched No. 12 burn.

Friday 14 March, 1941
I remember as the day went on, how No. 7 – it was a wide pend [a vehicle entrance from the street through a tenement block] which stretched to the street right

through to the back court – started filling up with dead bodies.

The rescue workers were putting them there so as anyone who was worried about missing relatives, went to the pend to see if they were there. Thank goodness I did not have to do that.

… We did not know where to go, we wanted away from the tenement buildings, which took quite a bashing on Thursday night, and thought if a bomb falls near our street the buildings will collapse, for our close was in a terrible state, there was a crack right up from the close to the top flat. My father decided we were going to Denny, as our house was in a terrible state we could not live in it. My mother, who had died many years before, came from Denny and we had some friends there.

By this time there was some transport put on to take people away, as most of the houses were uninhabitable. The people were in schools and church halls and the Red Cross were serving tea. Our close was declared unsafe and Agnes and me were not allowed up to our house to get our clothes, so we went to Nellie's house. Later my father persuaded a warden to let him go up to the house.

We lived two storeys up and he took out my trunk which was full of my things which I had saved for my house when I got married. He also took out my brother's radio-gram.

I do not know how he managed to get them down the stairs. That was two journeys he made up the stairs and the warden would not allow him to go back up. He left them in a park in Dunn Street.

We went to Denny and we were treated great by our friends, they made us very welcome, in fact two of them – Crissie and Oweny Grant – gave us their house and they went and stayed with her father. We could not have had better friends.

My father had arranged for a van to go to Clydebank, he was determined to get more of our things out as we only had the clothes we were wearing, but when he arrived at Pattison Street on Sunday, No. 11 was a mass of flames. He said he just stood and watched it burning and the tears ran down his face. It must have been terrible to see your life's work destroyed before your eyes.

My father never had a home of his own after that for he died before he was allocated a house and all we had were the two things he brought out. I know he was thinking of me when he saved my trunk and he knew John had saved hard to buy his radio-gram and he risked his life to get them out.

… We lost our home and most of our possessions, but the Haggerty family survived the Clydebank Blitz.

The official report into public behaviour during the raids said that morale was good, and it paid tribute to the quiet patience of people arranging accommodation afterwards. The chief topic of conversation – and a crucial factor in maintaining morale – was compensation for war damage. It also noted that:

There were no ladders from the top tenement land-ings to the high ceilings of Radnor Park tenements. The breakdown of water supply compelled the Fire Brigade and the Auxiliary Fire Service to confine their attention to the lower parts of the town.

However the report blamed local people for the extent of
the damage:

> the people themselves, by making adequate preparations,
> could have saved a half or more of destroyed Clydebank.

Nearly all the homes in Clydebank were damaged or
destroyed. At the outbreak of war Clydebank's population
was 45,000; after the Blitz it dropped to 2,000, although it
had climbed back up to 32,000 in 1945.

As a port, Plymouth in Devon was among the cities hit
by heavy and frequent raids. Choc Steed was a typist working for HQ South Western Command in Plymouth in
1940–41. She and Roy (who was in the Royal Navy) were
married in March 1941:

> After a week in Penzance we went to Dartmouth,
> where we intended spending our last week [of our
> honeymoon]. On the Saturday morning we heard on
> the radio that Plymouth had had a very bad blitz on
> the Thursday and Friday night, so we packed and left
> straight away …
>
> We had been away nearly two weeks and when we
> returned, the church where we were married was noth-
> ing but a shell. I believe we were the last couple to be
> married there. The restaurant where the reception was
> held and the photographers' were gone, as was practi-
> cally the whole of the centre of Plymouth. The whole
> town was devastated and firemen had come from miles
> around to tackle the blaze. Friends of ours who lived in
> Torrington in North Devon, 54 miles away, told us how
> they stood on Castle Hill and watched the glow in the

The centre of Plymouth in May 1941. After nearly a year of raids on the
city, entire blocks had been flattened, shops were boarded up and buildings
such as the church spire here were being repaired. This was typical of
the scenes in heavily bombed towns and city centres across the United
Kingdom. The white bands painted on telegraph poles would guide people
in the blackout.

sky over Plymouth, knowing that men from their families had gone with the brigade to help.

... People were going out into the lanes around Plymouth to sleep. Those who could spare the petrol took their cars, but others walked. Every evening hundreds of women and children could be seen walking along the roads. I took my Mother out and sometimes my Mother-in-law and sister-in-law came with us. We couldn't go every night – there wasn't enough petrol – but we managed three or four times a week. We left about 10.30 pm and returned about 5 am. We pulled the cars tight into the hedge and got what sleep we could. When we returned, my Mother would make us a cup of tea whilst I took the car to the garage – which was about half a mile away – and then we would go to bed for an hour or so before going to work. One night we were all in our cars, tight to the hedge, when suddenly a German plane appeared overhead and machine gunned straight down the lane. Fortunately no-one was hurt. It had been cloudy when we parked and we hadn't realised it was a full moon and that when it came out it would shine straight on us. We all moved across to the other side in case any more returning planes passed overhead but it was quiet for the rest of the night.

With its extensive shipbuilding industries, Belfast was vital to war production. It was the target of a massive raid on Easter Tuesday, 15 April 1941. Over 200 bombers came over the city. More than 1,000 people died – the biggest loss of life outside London during a night raid. Half the city's houses were destroyed. James Doherty, an air raid warden in the city, became one of 100,000 people out of a population of 425,000 who became homeless that night. He recalled later that the weather that day had been good and a German reconnaissance plane had been spotted flying over the city. At 10.45 p.m. the wailing sirens gave warning that enemy aircraft were approaching. The wardens who had stood by during the day were already at the post; others came hurrying in. James Doherty recorded that even those who had been on holiday had scarcely time to unpack before reporting for duty:

> Suddenly the city was illuminated by giant flares which floated down on parachutes. How can I find words to describe the intensity of the brilliance which tore through the darkness and bathed the city in a light greater than the sun at noon? Every building stood out in detail and we could see in all directions. Royal Avenue, North Street and Carlisle Circus were plainly visible, whereas a few seconds previously one could scarcely see an outstretched hand. The flares hung like giant electric lamps up in the sky. The flares themselves did not offer any threat to us but as we stood in the open bathed in their white light it was a disturbing and frightening experience. Frightening, because the city was exposed to the planes which could be hovering above like giant vultures waiting to dive on their prey. As I stood in the now fading light of the flares the thought came to me. Were the blackout, the smoke screens and hooded car lights of any use? At that moment it appeared to me that they were all totally ineffective.
>
> … Carlisle Circus and the Antrim Road showed signs of a heavy attack and my street was a shambles. What had been a row of neat terrace houses was now a mountain of rubble. I stood gazing at the mound which was once my home. I was dazed and frightened, thinking about

my family, my father, my mother and sister ... When I had spoken to them about taking shelter they often said that they would prefer to stay in the house rather than go to the shelters. Our shelters were far from being suitable places to spend a night. Doors were never fitted to them and they had lain neglected since they were built. Local residents used them as places for dumping rubbish and throughout the city they were often used as public conveniences. Overall they were dark, evil smelling, airless dungeons. Knowing the general feeling with which the public regarded the shelters only increased my panic. In a daze I made my way to the post, almost afraid to hear the news I so much wanted to know. I met some wardens who assured me that my family were safe ... The more active of us decided to form a type of flying squad to investigate the various sites of damage and do what we could for the injured or partially trapped.

... Our plan was simple; we would move from site to site, treat the wounded, effect any possible rescue with our picks and crowbars and attack any fires which we thought we could control. It was a hit and run operation but we had to achieve something in what appeared to be a hopeless situation ... Burke Street had disappeared; not a house was standing. The death toll here was high, as it was in this entire area. Everywhere we went we met with death, and the horror of it all was that the dead outnumbered the injured. I knew these people well and I had often chatted with them as I passed through the streets on patrol and the children would share their sweets or walk along with me. Now it was heartbreaking to think of their mangled bodies below those mounds of rubble. This was the hardest part of the warden's job ... As I came in contact with manifest panic and fear, I was glad and thankful that I had become involved with A.R.P.

After two hectic days:

we made it back to the post about 2 o'clock in the morning. My feet felt as if they were cut to pieces. I asked someone to pull off my boots and I lay down on the floor and fell fast asleep. I woke early, feeling refreshed. Others had joined me during the night on the floor and some were sleeping on the benches. It was a comforting sight. I was proud to be a part of this group of great fellows. There was no gas and we made a fire with sticks, and brewed a pot of tea. Someone produced a piece of bread. It was stale, but we spread it liberally with jam. There was no milk to be bought and what we had was sour, so we took the tea black. It was a rough breakfast but it suited the circumstances. There were at least a dozen of us living at the post. Our families had gone away or our houses were destroyed or badly damaged. I knew I would have to get some clean clothes and a bath and a shave. I could not go through another day in my present state. We went out on an early patrol. It was about 7 o'clock and as we moved through the streets the locals greeted us. Other wardens had kept contact with them during the night and like ourselves they did not go to bed but just dozed off sitting in their chairs. It was good to see them looking so settled and not frightened. The first night in the ghost town had passed quietly. On our return to the post I decided to go down to the old house and make a determined effort to rescue some of my clothes before the day really started. I was joined by about six or seven of the gang and we moved off like a squad of navies, carrying ropes, picks and shovels. The upper storeys and staircase had collapsed but I located what I thought was my bedroom in the heart of a mountain of rubble. The whole row of houses had collapsed like a pack of cards when a parachute mine exploded at the rear in Lincoln Avenue. We started to clear the debris and the gang worked as if a life depended on their efforts. The idea of digging for my clothes and other belongings was great fun for them and excitement grew as we unearthed the wardrobe and a chest of drawers. As they saw it, they thought of it as digging for buried treasure. The wardrobe and drawers were twisted and broken but I was excited and relieved as we pulled them out; but then sadness struck me. This was all that remained. This was all I possessed. We carried them to the post, which was to be my home for the next two months until I was able to get a place and bring my family together again. At the time I did not think much of it but later when I settled down in my new home my thoughts wandered to my books, stamp collections and a rare and beautiful collection of postcards and autographs of a grand selection of European celebrities in pre-war Europe. I was a keen Esperantist and I collected many small mementos from all over the world. Fellow Esperantists sent me autographs and stamps, some rare, some ordinary, but they all helped to build up a very picturesque collection which I treasured … The Nazis did not approve of the Esperanto movement and its idea of peace and brotherhood. Hundreds of Esperantists were executed or disappeared into concentration camps. I lost some personal friends in this way. I never met them but a close friendship had grown up between us.

During April there were two major raids on London, on 16 and 19 April – 'the Wednesday raid' and 'the Saturday raid,' as they became known. These diversions from the main strategy may have been retaliation for recent heavy RAF raids on Berlin.

On the night of 16 April an estimated 450 bombers flew over London. They dropped 446 tons of high-explosive bombs, and 150 tonnes of incendiaries, mostly to the south and over the city centre.

Eric Wilton, a member of the Royal Observer Corps in Bromley, south-east London, wrote afterwards about the night:

The Church House building, which had housed the Observer Corps in Bromley since the beginning of the War, was totally destroyed. B Crew were not on duty that evening; but many B Crew members were also members of F, the Duty Crew, and played their part in the losing fight against the flames.

The first waves of raiders reached London shortly after 9 pm. It had been abundantly clear that from the pressure of tracks on radar that this was to be an attack of the first magnitude.

At 21.35 a heavy bomb struck the Parish Church, some 200 yards from the centre, demolishing it completely except for a portion of the tower. Most of the windows of the Church House were broken by the blast, and the heavy stones from the old walls of the church were flung into the surrounding gardens, creating indescribable confusion. At the same time, thousands of incendiary bombs fell on the Church House and other buildings in the vicinity. Plotting continued while the fire picket climbed on to the roof and endeavoured to cope with the fires which were already rapidly gaining ground amongst the rafters. Some 16 incendiaries were either extinguished, or thrown clear of the building. However, there were others which could not be reached, and in spite of every effort, within 20 minutes the whole roof was fiercely ablaze and seemed likely to collapse. No fire engine could hope to reach the Church House, because the road leading past the church was blocked with debris. In any case, as was usual in concentrated raids of this type, the town water supply was quite inadequate to cope with the innumerable fires that were now blazing on all sides.

In these circumstances there was no alternative but to abandon the Centre. Bowen the acting Duty Controller, gave orders for the crew to leave in small parties, each man taking with him as much moveable equipment as he could carry. The first party to leave was at once to man the emergency Centre, situated in the old telephone exchange, some three hundred yards distant. Plotting and telling was to be continued by the remainder of the crew, so as to avoid, if possible, any break in the continuity of the work. This was important, both because of the intensity of the raid, and the number of night fighters that were operating. Half-blinded with smoke, plotters and tellers continued their work. Very shortly, large portions of the roof began to fall in. The first floor immediately above the operations room became a raging inferno. Reluctantly, Bowen gave the final order to abandon the Centre. As he followed the last member of his crew out of the building he could hear the ground floor ceilings crashing one by one as the great weight of the flaming roof bore down on them.

It was not, after all, possible to get the emergency Centre fully working before the old operations room was abandoned. But thanks to the devotion of the Duty Crew and the courage of their Controller, the lapse of time during which the raid went unplotted was only a matter of minutes. The back of the old telephone exchange, in which the Crew were now housed, was on fire. So was the Vicarage next door. A small party of volunteers tackled both these outbreaks, and shortly had them under control. By a quarter to eleven, when G Crew took over, plotting and telling were proceeding smoothly on such [telephone] lines as had not been destroyed by the fury of the flames and high explosive.

The Wednesday raid killed 1,180 and badly injured 2,230, more than any previous attack. Eighteen hospitals and thirteen churches were damaged and over sixty public buildings affected, including (again) the Houses of Parliament and the Law Courts. At St Paul's, a heavy high-explosive bomb fell through the north transept, causing great damage, but the dome remained intact. At one point all the Southern Railway termini were closed. Several telephone exchanges were damaged, and gas supplies badly affected, but on the whole the utility services did not suffer as might have been expected.

Three nights later, on the 19th, about 350 bombers returned, concentrating this time on the docks and the East End, dropping parachute mines and incendiaries. Casualty figures were again high, with over 1,200 killed and 1,000 seriously injured.

After these raids, the Luftwaffe returned to attacks on the ports.

On 7 May, two months after the attack on Clydebank, the town of Greenock, further along the banks of the River Clyde, was targeted.

The report by the fire-master, A.S. Pratten, written on 16 May, noted that co-operation and reinforcements from other brigades had been crucial:

In the very early stages of the raid a stick of high explosive bombs struck the Ardgowan Distillery and fired a warehouse containing about three million gallons of whisky. A tremendous body of fire was almost immediately generated and, from this time on, the area was systematically bombed, many neighbouring premises being set on fire. The Fire service was powerless to control the initial fire, in the circumstances, and the situation rapidly depreciated as succeeding buildings were fired. The raid then became more widespread and a serious fire situation developed.

In the early stages of the raid, the water mains were so badly damaged as to be useless for the larger areas of fire and it was necessary to relay water from the harbours and from aqueducts at the back of the town ...

The telephone service was of negligible value during the raid. Telephonic communication with the auxiliary station nearest to the main fire area failed completely at about 01.45. At about this time all telephones failed, to be restored and fail again later.

But overall ... The local Fire Brigade organisation stood up to the 'blitz' remarkably well. It was overwhelmed by the number and size of the fires which were started in so short a time, but the organisation did not collapse and when reinforcements started to arrive the issue was never in doubt. The control organisation worked smoothly and well and was proved to be capable of dealing with an even greater raid. A marked feature of the whole experience has been the ready co-operation and willingness to assist on the part of other brigades. In particular, the Firemasters of both Glasgow and Paisley, and the Regional Fire Brigades Inspector, have been most helpful and this has had a decided effect upon the problems facing the local service.

In preparing for the bombers' return the following night, lights were placed a few miles outside the town and were mainly successful in directing them away from Greenock.

As the largest port area on the western coast, Liverpool and Birkenhead had regular and heavy raids – more than any city apart from London. The Blitz on the city began in August 1940 and continued until May 1941.

This letter was written by Kathleen Hanlon, most of it while she sat in the family Anderson shelter ('The Dive'), to her mother in the Isle of Man. The shop she refers to, where she worked as a dispensing chemist, was in the Scotland Road area of Liverpool, about 2½ miles away:

The Dive Thursday Dear Ma,
Thanks for the letter. I nearly got my ticket to 'Kingdom Come' tonight. Have just landed home after a most exciting time. I had just left the shop when the sirens went & the guns started almost immediately & then I heard Jerry. I kept on walking however as there were no shelters near, &

was just going up the Valley when – whistle – bang on my left & whistle – bang on my right & Chadwick Mount church seemed to go up in the air & come down all round me. It was so sudden, nobody had a chance to take cover. The trams were stopped immediately and everyone turfed off them, but he dropped no more near us. When I had recovered, I discovered that the church was still standing but not a window was left in it, the bomb must have dropped at the back of it. The blast blew a man over on the other side of the road from me & rocked a tram a few yards ahead of me. (There's the 'all clear' 8 o'clock.) A house in Kirkdale Vale got the 1st one, & there was a white powder all over the road, don't know what it was. About a dozen wardens came flying along & started banging at all the doors to see if the people inside the houses were OK. I heard someone shout 'burst the door open', that must have been the house that was hit, it hadn't collapsed, so it must have got it at the back. I hope I never get anything closer than these two, gosh, I was scared.

Kept on walking like Felix & discovered a fire in a house off Walton Lane, flames coming out of the windows – must have been an incendiary. Jerry was still buzzing round but I kept on the move & managed to get to Cherry Lane when the guns started full blast. I turned down Cherry Lane & tacked myself on to a man & the two of us trotted along as far as the Hermitage when we decided it was a bit too hot so we stood in the doorway there until the guns cooled off a bit. There is a mobile gun here which runs round the roads & it goes off with a terrific crack, not a bang, & it was busy near us. Then we decided to do a hop to the shelter by the Ebenezer, so we took to our heels & flew along the Drive among the bangs & flashes, the sky was just lit up. The shelter was full when we got there but we squeezed in the doorway. I wasn't there long before things went quiet & I made another hop home. I can't realize yet that I'm still in one piece. It was an awful experience …

Hope you don't mind the bad writing & all the mistakes, but I guess my nerves aren't quite steady yet, & I'm in the house now, (Auntie Mag & I came out of the Dive when the 'all clear' went, but she has gone back now) so I'm listening to every sound outside even though there's no raid on.

I wrote to Pa on Monday night & told him that it had been pretty quiet here lately. I had hardly sealed his letter when Jerry dropped two time bombs which sounded very near here, but turned out to be in Gt Mersey St & Boundary St. One of them went off with an awful bang about 3.30 am & wrecked a Methodist Church. Another bomb scored a direct hit on a church school in Fonthill Rd behind Stanley Hospital. I went along & had a look at it on Tuesday night. It's just a heap of bricks & rubbish.

That umbrella shop in Clayton Sq., which was wrecked has a big notice outside – Demolition by Adolf Hitler & Co – reconstructions by Tysons. That's all for now.
Love Kath

Hospitals in cities vulnerable to air raids had evacuated many patients and staff but remained open, initially to deal with air raid casualties. In the London area, hospitals were coordinated under the Emergency Medical Service. Its success had a major influence on the National Health Service, created just after the war in 1948. John Robert Lee, an Australian-born surgeon and author of the following paper, was 67 when he joined the EMS at the start of the war. He worked in a hospital in Battersea, London:

British Medical Journal April 19th 1941
EXPERIENCES IN THE RECEPTION AND
TREATMENT OF AIR RAID CASUALTIES BY
JOHN ROBERT LEE, M.D., B.S., F.R.C.S.
These notes cover a period of two months when intensive enemy air raids occurred over London. During this period 227 patients came under my care and supervision. Many of us have seen and treated badly injured civilians brought to hospital as the result of road, railway, or works accidents in peacetime. It seems to me, however, that only those who have had to deal with victims of air raids can conceive the appalling condition and appearance of many of these patients on their arrival in hospital.

A sight which must be seen to be appreciated fully is the almost indescribably filthy condition of many who evidently had been clean and well clad. A patient is brought to the receiving ward with her clothes cut and torn to shreds, her hair singed, filled with dirt, and matted with blood and cement dust, her body and limbs covered with grit and oil, her face blackened, bruised, and bleeding, her eyes, nose, lips, and ears filled with dirt, her head bandaged, and her limbs immobilized by improvised splints at the first-aid post. Truly it is a picture not easy to forget.

After triage, he describes:

'Our Routine'
... The patient was at once assured he would be safe and well cared for; those who were distressed because they

could not see owing to dirt, swelling, or eye injury were told not to fear going blind. Their eyes were thoroughly cleansed and castor-oil instilled at once, and their lips and mouths were also cleaned. The patients then had a cup of fresh tea with sugar. Anti-tetanic serum was given to all the wounded. Brief notes were written and any such treatment was recorded on the case sheet, especially if morphine had been administered at the first-aid post. The patient was then sent to the ward. The nursing staff carried out their duties efficiently, often working on far into the night after a long day. Patients well enough were removed from the stretchers and put to bed.

After detailing procedures for pain relief, hygiene, anaesthesia, dressings, and the benefits of having two surgeons work simultaneously on any patient with multiple wounds, Lee describes the successful treatment of a girl aged 15, who:

apparently had a large glass tumbler blown through her left shoulder …

Her left upper limb was attached to her body by its vessels, nerves, and a band of skin about two inches wide.

Her condition was desperate. The huge wounds in front of and behind what was her shoulder were filled freely with glycerin and iodine while resuscitation measures were being carried out. After thirty-six hours she was taken to the theatre and attended to as described herein. Portions of her coat and other clothes, with dirt and debris, were removed from the wounds, then more glycerin-and-iodine solution was constantly applied. Gas gangrene was feared, as cultures showed the presence of B. welchii. A dose of anti-gas gangrene serum was given.

She did not develop gas gangrene. At the end of five weeks she was able to move her elbow, forearm, wrist, thumb, and fingers well. The wounds were almost healed, and her general condition was good.

Many patients had literally scores of wounds on the face, body, hands, and legs. Excision was out of the question. These were treated by having the wounds curetted with gauze soaked in glycerin and iodine. On the face no dressings were used. The wounds were frequently painted. The small scabs were shed in about a week. Multiple wounds of the limbs were painted, and a sterile towel was placed so as to prevent contact with the bed-clothes. All such wounds healed in less than a fortnight with very little scarring. By this method healing takes place rapidly under a scab with little or no pus, usually in less than a fortnight. There are no repeated painful dressings. The growing tissues are not damaged.

The circulation and local nervous mechanism are not interfered with by bandages or other material placed around a limb. Every effort was made to avoid amputation, usually with satisfactory result ...

Visitors were allowed freely, but were warned that there were to be 'no tears' while in the wards.

The blindness he mentions was a frequent, if usually temporary, problem. In May 1942, H.R. Clothier, by now in the RAF and stationed in Harborne near Birmingham, could speak from experience:

We had raids regularly but there was one night that will always be remembered by me. The sirens had gone and the horrible droning of heavy bombers had started.

Then came the thud of bombs not far distant, and then we saw incendiaries dropping in the gardens. We all rushed out to put them out and I totally forgot all my drills and tried to clout one with a spade. A great shower of light came before my eyes and I couldn't see. I fumbled my way indoors shouting out 'I'm blind!' Someone came and attended to me … and slowly I began to see again. It is wonderful to find that you have not been blinded and still have your sight. I shall never forget the relief.

Crime continued to rise. As people slept in the public shelters – especially in London Tube stations – pickpockets made off with their valuables. Others burgled the homes of people they knew would be in the shelters. Across the country, organised gangs of criminals, some wearing ARP uniforms, came to clear houses. In 1942, at Dover on the south coast, Chief Inspector Percy Datlen said:

> In cases where there are several houses bombed out in one street, the looters have systematically gone through the lot. Carpets have been stripped from the floors, stair carpets have been removed: they have even taken away heavy mangles, bedsteads and complete suites of furniture. We believe it is the greatest organized looting that has yet taken place and many front line citizens who have returned to their homes to carry on their essential jobs there are facing severe financial difficulties as a result of the work of the gang.

The WVS (Women's Voluntary Services) was founded in 1938 to bring women into ARP services. It had over one million members during the Second World War and supported people during and after air raids.

Anne Lee Michell was in the WVS. Born in Highgate in 1908, she and her husband Frank Lee Michell (referred to here as Mike) lived near Wellington in Somerset with their daughters Sarah and Caroline (Toots). Mike was in the Home Guard.

Anne's wartime diaries include this account of her visit to Plymouth as part of the WVS Queen's Messenger Convoys. These convoys of lorries, driven by WVS members, arrived in bombed areas within hours of major raids, to help feed survivors and rescue workers:

Saturday 3rd May 1941

12.45 Babs rushed out and caught me to say [we're] to head for Plymouth to cook for and drive the Queen's Messenger Convoy for food. Rushed home to pack then drove to Plymouth with Babs, Mrs Langford and Mrs Walker. Found lovely blue and fawn vans on the car park in blitzed suburb of Plymouth and drove one to Tavistock where they're [parked] for night. Muddled gears and held up the whole convoy! Dinner at pub in Tavistock then long moonlit drive over Dartmoor and Ivybridge(?) where a relative of Mrs Langford put us up. Whole day completely unreal!

Sunday 4th May 1941

Get up at cock crow an hour earlier owing to double summertime. Lovely early drive to Tavistock, found the right way and did it quicker. Drove my van to Plymouth and did day's work stirring soup, cutting bread and butter etc. Whole affair is rather a muddle, no-one to organise work, masses of helpers doing nothing, etc. Convoy = 2 kitchens, 2 stores, 2 water carts, 3 canteens. Canteens go on distributing food around Plymouth but we were not sent. Drove back to Tavistock. Van's nice to drive now I am used to them.

5th May

Drove over Dartmoor so lovely in the early morn, frost in the meadows and moors all misty. Such a hard day's work today, never sat down at all. Got sent out with canteen amid frightful rubbish, ruined homes, soldiers doing demolition. Very glad of tea – dust so awful. Could never have imagined such scenes – nothing left of whole streets but twisted girders and rubble. People so pathetic, especially the kids. Terribly tired by the evening but drove back somehow.

6th May – our last day in Plymouth, glad as I am, so dirty from the smoke of our Dixies [cooking pot], and stray incendiary from raid last night lit a smelly Dixie very nicely! Was sent out again and soon sold out of soup and food, so drove home through ruined Plymouth and saw most of it. Shall never forget these three days. Hoped to be relieved from Bristol but no-one came so had to drive convoy back to Tavistock as usual and come home from here. Got in at 9.30 dead tired longing for Mike but had awful row. He has had hypoglycaemia … as he forgot to take his sugar on Home Guard. Told him off, he furious and me too tired to care. Wot a day – prayed a bomb would fall on me when Huns come over!

Belfast had four raids between 7 April and 6 May. Rumours filled the vacuum created by official news blackouts. On 7 May 1941, Mollie Wilson wrote to her parents:

AC W Wilson
c/o Guard Room Rudloe Manor Box,
Worcs

Dearest Mother and Daddy (4.20 am)
I haven't heard from either of you for some little time now, and am just a bit worried in case the latest raid over Belfast interfered with your routine in any way. Have you been called up for the Civil Nursing or anything Mother? You see, I have only heard second hand about the raid, and though I have tried very hard I can only find very little information about it. In fact, I haven't seen it in print at all. One of the G.P.O. men, knowing I was from Ireland, told me about it, and that it was very serious, with huge numbers of casualties. So that is all I know. If it is true you will both be very busy, so don't worry about me. Letter cards will be all right, or a post card now and then, till the emergency passes. But above all, please don't work too hard.

There is a swift reply and she writes again:

10th May 1941
Dearest Mother
Your letter arrived yesterday just after I had posted mine to you. I hope you won't think me silly for beginning to worry. But after the raid so many people asked me so many times if I had heard from home, that they began

to make me wonder. Everything is okay now though and my only trouble is that you may be annoyed with me for being a little panicky. I'm so glad the damage to Belfast was so slight. You see, stories over here get so exaggerated, and this girl back from leave said that the city was practically flat. So I'll tell her next time I see her.

The port of Kingston upon Hull was strategically important and was an easily identified location along the route to other places. It was hit in targeted raids but also German bombers who could not find their intended targets would find Hull instead. Fewer than 7 per cent of its homes escaped damage from the raiders. The first raids, in March 1941, killed 100 people. Four hundred more died in two raids between 7/8 and 8/9 May. Shortly afterwards, Phillip Chignell visited his friend Arthur, who lived in the Charterhouse in the city centre. He wrote to his sister:

Arthur is now living the life of a troglodyte … He has his bed in an underground dugout, where he keeps his books and his wireless. He is safe enough there from anything except a direct hit … I had a cup of tea with Arthur in front of the kitchen fire and every window was broken and out and every door open and uncloseable and half the ceiling down on the floor. Just the same in every room, broken pictures, broken furniture and glass lying about everywhere, things crack under your feet as you walk about and all the time you feel the house is going to tumble down on top of you. Whilst we were having tea an unexploded bomb or a workmen's blast went off quite close and the whole place rocked. Just over the garden wall is St Phillip's church, the rectory belonging to this church and the Alexandra theatre, all close together. A bomb smashed the lot up. The theatre with its very big spiral tower fell right over the vicarage. Canon Sedgewick, the vicar and a friend of mine, has not been heard of up to now. Mrs Sedgewick was rescued from the wreckage. It is only a few days ago that I stood at this very corner talking to Canon and Mrs Sedgewick. A barrage balloon had broken away from close by and the trailing wire rope had cut the canon's telephone wire … Canon Sedgewick then told me that he had just returned from burying six people who had lost their lives in one of the raids. Well? Whose turn next? This is just what it amounts to.

… I went into Hull on the Friday morning and saw what had happened. The raid attack had hit the centre of the city very badly. It looked as though a big earthquake had occurred. Houses down in every direction. Streets blocked with masses of stones and bricks and girders and goodness knows what else. I never thought I should live to see such a sight. I went in on my bicycle. Time after time I was turned off my road and sent up a bye street to get to my destination how I liked, so long as I did not go along that particular road the policeman or the soldier was guarding.

… The latest idea seems to be to drop a parachute, it does not matter very much where it drops so long as it drops somewhere. As soon as it touches the ground or anything in the way of a building there is the devil of an explosion and every house in the vicinity is wrecked. A tank of oil is released and at once ignites and if that is not hell my imagination fails me …

Someday Hull will recover and live again. Just now it has received a knockout blow. This sort of thing was rather expected right at the beginning of the war, when it did not come we all began to think it never would come. Well, the same thing cannot exactly happen again. We are never likely to see the city burning again as it did that night. There is not the stuff to burn.

Just after 11 o'clock on the night of 10/11 May 1941, the Luftwaffe returned to London under a full moon. Around 550 aircraft took part in a five-hour attack, mainly on the east and south-eastern districts and the City, although damage was inflicted on seventy-five boroughs. This was the last and the heaviest bombing raid across the capital.

Nearly 1,500 were killed and 1,800 seriously injured – the highest number of casualties for any night of the Blitz. In the centre of London, 2,200 fires were started, destroying the Chamber of the House of Commons and damaging Westminster Abbey and School, as well as the British Museum, the Law Courts, the War Office, the Royal Mint, Mansion House and the Tower of London. These fires were fought by 2,500 pumps including reinforcements from outside London. Even so, it was not until 5.30 p.m. on the following day that the fires were all under control.

This was the Luftwaffe's final large-scale raid on London. Five weeks later, on 22 June 1941, Hitler invaded Russia in a surprise attack. Many believe this last and heaviest raid on London was a diversion.

It marked the end of the Big Blitz.

BAEDEKER RAIDS AND THE 'LITTLE BLITZ'

By 1942 the Luftwaffe was concentrating its power on the war against Russia. From February that year the RAF was gaining the upper hand over Britain. On 28 March, the RAF attacked the German port of Lübeck, dropping high-explosives and incendiaries on the old town, which was mainly made up of medieval wooden buildings. The raid caused widespread destruction and left 1,000 dead. Hitler ordered reprisals against Britain's oldest and most beautiful cities in what are loosely termed the 'Baedeker raids'. One view is that these raids were so named because they were thought to have been planned using a Baedeker travel guide. It was also reported that Hitler had said the raids would cause the Baedeker guide to Britain to be re-written. There were two phases to these raids. During the first, the Luftwaffe bombed Exeter, Bath, Norwich and York; Canterbury was the target in the second.

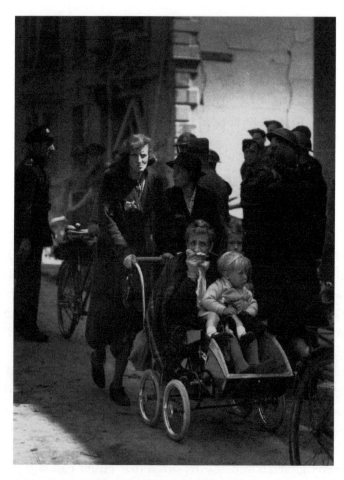

Survivors hurry away from the devastation in the ancient city of
Canterbury on 2 June 1942, the day after the city's heaviest raid. Teams
of firewatchers on the cathedral's roof saved it from serious damage by
clearing away incendiary bombs. Many of the city's other ancient buildings
were destroyed and 115 people were killed during 135 raids on the city.
Picture by Fred Ramage, courtesy of Hulton Getty

By this time, WAAF Mollie Wilson was on an RAF station near Bath. She wrote later:

On summer evenings, when German bombers came droning over, thirty, fifty maybe in formation, we stood in the open gazing up at the black crosses on their wings, watching while one or maybe two of our own few aircraft took off to intercept. Sometimes our boys would shoot down two or three, before they crashed themselves, outnumbered and outmatched. German and British planes would spiral down together in a trail of smoke. For weeks, our half-completed camp was strewn with wreckage hauled in by salvage crews and you mourned for boys you'd known who died that day. When Bath itself was bombed, civilians came streaming out, taking refuge in the village where we had our billets, sleeping, many of them, in the hedges, deeply shocked, unwilling to return. Bath was an 'open city', full of treasures, and they'd taken it for granted the war would never reach their very door. Surprisingly, the bombers never found our camp or never touched it anyway, but after a while, when things were going badly for the country and secure communications were absolutely vital, they built an operations complex down more than a hundred feet in caves that stretch halfway to Bristol. Hours were long and hectic, and it was part of our job to pass on air raid warnings, yellow, purple, red. Attacks were plotted on a large map table and you estimated threatened areas in an arc around the planes, advancing with them.

F. Wilfred Willway, a doctor and ARP officer in Bristol, was sent to Bath during the Baedeker raids of 25 and 26 April 1942. Shortly after, he wrote in the *British Medical Journal* about the attacks on both those cities:

In the winter of 1940–41 Bristol received its average share of air raids. I was active in all save one of these and learnt first-hand lessons. As the winter of 1941–42 approached we were all keyed up to face the bombardments that never came.

Instead raids were made on smaller neighbouring towns, notably Weston-Super-Mare and Bath. It is obviously possible to view a raid on a neighbouring city with considerable detachment.

Such vision may be useful, and I had the good fortune to assist in the 'good-neighbour policy' in all these raids. In each case we spent part of the time in the 'blitzed city' and part of the time organizing in the 'rescuing city.' This was possible as the raids were repeated on the second night in each town. On the whole the good-neighbour system worked well, but it is felt that many improvements could be made ... Admittedly some of it is painfully obvious, but most British cities found that it took actual bombs to drive the lessons home!

Communications

... In the case of the Weston raid, phone communication with Bristol was good though the line was sadly overworked (raid excitement) and messages were repeated unnecessarily – for example, a request for more sulphapyridine was separately phoned up by four officials.

In the Bath raids communication was bad. (This is written in terms of the hospital personally visited.) I arrived there, at 2 p.m. on the day after the first raid. (I was then leading a surgical team under orders from the Group M.O.) We saw cases and operated till 12 midnight, staying at the hospital for the second raid. At 4.45 a.m. casualties were again arriving.

Since leaving Bristol we had been unable to contact Bristol or the other Bath hospitals. The sole contact was the visit of a dispatch rider at 4 p.m. on the first day. We had then been there only two hours and were in no position to know what extra help might be needed, as the problem had only just been surveyed – e.g., some 60 casualties in an unfamiliar hospital with facilities for two teams to operate. At that time we were not au fait with the laundry position or the drug and dressing position.

At 6 o'clock on the morning of the second raid I returned to Bristol in my own car to obtain further aid. Clearly this was wrong. It should not be necessary to detach a surgeon to act as a dispatch rider. It is now obvious that when the dispatch rider called at 4 p.m., the aid I should have requested was the honour of a further inspection at, say, 10 p.m., when we would have understood the situation better. We should then have known enough to appeal for rations. The large team I brought was deplorably fed, yet it worked for 24 hours except for a 4-hour break, and most of its members had been up and doing in Bristol for 14 hours previously. Good warm drinks and substantial meals are necessary for the nurses, doctors, and others in such circumstances.

When Should Help be Sent?
The hospital in the bombed city may be cleverly organized, but it will need help.

If it is so staffed that it does not require help in an air raid, then it is over-staffed and is wasteful of man-power, and doctors should be requisitioned from it for military service! … In one city that was helped – on the arrival of the rescuing team the whole resident M.O. staff of the hospital retired to bed – a sensible manoeuvre.

What Type of Help Should be Sent?
I have firm views on this subject, and they conflict to some extent with E.M.S. authority as stated in the 'Red Book.' However, I will venture to dogmatize …

The 'Shock Troops' Team:
The first help to be sent should be strong parties of medical students with a few sensible housemen. These I consider my shock troops – they are 'go-anywhere-do-anything men.' They will give a blood transfusion, take a blood pressure, shave a head, write notes (vital: I have seldom seen a 'General' write a note), put out a small fire, act as stretcher-bearers, give simple anaesthetics, form a minor surgical team, and generally do the ten-thousand-and-one things that 'proper doctors' seem to find beneath them. The supreme pull of the big city over the smaller is not in the greater excellence of its consulting staff but in the number of its medical students. Where possible I would include in the shock division that other salt of the earth, an almoner with her clerk. This division, warmly clothed (Battle dress for shock troops is old clothes, a torch, pencil and pad, and a pair of dressing scissors) and well fed, should be on the road within 1 hour of news of 'the incident.' …

Surgical Teams:
The surgical teams that seem to be so beloved of the E.M.S. can well leave at a much later hour, say

breakfast-time. They are not needed in the first few hours unless the stricken area has no surgeon at all (highly improbable), in which case a surgeon must leave with the shock troops. Most casualties can well do with a few hours' rest; the few 'vitally urgent' cases can be dealt with by the local surgeons, who, having withstood the night's raid, will appreciate relief at 9 a.m. to see to their own homes, etc., but who do not want relief at 5 a.m. or 6 a.m ...

The wise surgeon will pack his own kit; every surgeon will have his own fancy, but in air raids the best surgeon is the one who needs the least tools. I have a passion for taking razors (and a student to hone them) and nail-brushes ...

It is well to carry goods for one's own comfort – e.g., a theatre suit, gum boots, and a mackintosh. The visiting surgeon who bothers the visited hospital for these things is not helping – he's wasting time, energy, and tempers. Ideally, a surgical team should be relieved every 8 to 10 hours, otherwise efficiency will fall off ...

Nursing Relief:
This is important, and requires nice judgment and execution. A two-nights-running air raid is a heavy test of the usually busy, usually under-nursed general hospital. If to the admission of numbers of casualties be added minor bomb damage (windows blown in, no black-out, etc.) and noisy excitement in the daytime precluding rest, then the strain on the night nurses is heavy. We tried the experiment of exchanging units of nurses between the central city and the bombed town, thus providing a 'quiet night'. This needs much arranging and nice timing when

all hospitals are working full out with minimal staffs. Two experiences in practice are related, and are instructive:

Twenty nurses were sent at 9 p.m. to the Weston General Hospital after the second night's raid (obviously no one knew if a third night's raid would occur). These nurses were courteously received and were distributed among the wards; during the night the local nurses were each given 4 hours off duty and their work thus lightened. Had a raid occurred the augmented staff could easily have shared the work. (A similar exchange of house-surgeons is desirable.) A similar party of 20 nurses were sent to another hospital, where the matron had already been advised to expect them. They were met on arrival, told they were not wanted, and sent back crestfallen to Bristol. What a lack of imagination and tact! The hospital in question did not even notify this action to the A.R.P. organizer, with the result that next day a bus was sent to fetch back nurses who had been returned the night before! These contrary experiences merely confirm the need for good planning.

Lily Pearson lived in York and was caught up in the Baedeker raid on the night of 28 April. Afterwards, she moved to a temporary address outside the city, from where she wrote to her aunt:

Dorothy & I were alone in the lounge when the raids came. The first thing we heard was the siren, then incendiary bombs dropping on the back bed. The bedroom was immediately on fire, & we turned on the bath taps, got buckets to throw water on the fire and ourselves, until we were soaked, but the flames were out. The bombs however were still under the bed, which is a low divan, & is too heavy for us to turn over. We had to act quickly I assure you. We went downstairs, it was blowing a gale outside, all York seemed to be on fire, flames & bombs were everywhere. We put 3 out in the front garden, & 3 in the street, then called 2 soldiers to help us with the bed. They put the whole bed, mattress & all, through the window, where it remains, a burnt wreck, & then we put the bombs out with sand. By that time the big bombs were coming down all around. My brother Raffael was out, putting fires out, with the rest of the men & the soldiers who are billeted in some of the houses. It was just like a nightmare, they dive bombed us, & machine gunned, the house was frightful. We stayed in the kitchen, being the smallest & safest place, while the whole place rocked, while roofs crashed & glass, & houses were hit all round. Raffael saved 2 houses from the fire, & we saved ours, but the nice crescent is no more. Huge fires engulfed whole houses. About 16 people, all acquaintances & some friends, were killed round about. About 5 houses out of 15 remain & they are damaged. Raffael's is like ours, roof mostly off, windows nearly all gone, including a lovely coloured one, & ceilings down. The bedroom, newly decorated, is burnt, & simply a mass of wet sand, & burnt rags, & walls splattered with molten metal from the bomb. We didn't get burnt at all, but we had to keep putting our faces in water, as the fumes & flames were choking. Other streets are almost as bad as ours, the whole half of the town right out of the suburbs is bad, there are thousands homeless.

We meet dozens of friends every time we go to York from here, who haven't a stitch left & only borrowed

clothes. Everyone is helping everyone else though, & we
had a good stock of clothing and all kinds of things from
the American Red Cross, & bedding for hostels for the
homeless, & I can assure you it is very much appreciated.
Our house was untenable, & I had offers of homes from
quite a few places. Meanwhile Bert, in the nursing home,
was, with the other patients, taken to the underground
shelter. They had fire bombs on the roof & time bombs in
the garden, but otherwise safe. He was very worried about
us though, until we went along early next morning. We
decided as Bert was due to leave, to come here to friends,
so they brought him out by car. We are 8 miles from York,
& it is so peaceful & quite lovely. River & woods round
about, & Bert is getting better quickly. The roof is already
back on our house, but we shan't return yet. I feel I couldn't
go back for a while. The street is roped off as traffic would
shake what remains. Only a few people are living there, it
looks so desolate & horrible. We can stay here just as long
as we like, but shall go back sometime I expect … street,
Guildhall & station caught it badly. Penley's Grove street
was quite untouched I think. We are so looking for the
end of the war. I do hope you won't come any nearer to it
than you have done so far. I pray that you & all your family
will keep safe through it all.

I will write you again soon with all news from here, &
I hope you will get this one anyway.
Once more, very many thanks for my 'Readers Digest'.
With love to you both from Dorothy & Bert & myself,
Your loving niece, Lily

RAF raids on Cologne on 22–23 April and Rostock on
23–24 April are thought to have provoked retaliatory

Luftwaffe attacks on Canterbury on 31 May, 2 June and 6 June 1942.

Schoolgirl Pam Cleverley (née Jordan) wrote later:

In 1942 I passed the scholarship to go to Simon Langton Girls' Grammar School in Canterbury and in June of that year we spent the night in our Morrison table shelter listening to the blitz on Canterbury. One of the buildings destroyed was the school to which I was supposed to go in the September. For the first term we shared the boy's school building which was untouched. One week we went from 9 am until 1 pm and the next week from 1 pm to 5 pm. It was a half hour bus journey from Herne Bay, which was fine until the cinema in Canterbury showed 'Gone with the Wind' and the performance ended just after 5 pm, which meant we couldn't get on the buses until about 6 pm. No mobile phones then, very few phones at all, so our parents must have worried. In January 1943 we finally found accommodation – the local psychiatric hospital. The patients had all been evacuated to Devon. As you can imagine the premises were not very suitable and the first few weeks must have been a nightmare for the staff. Directly you closed a door it locked, so the janitor spent his entire time rushing round with the master key. We had great fun jumping in the padded cells, until the head had them locked.

I spent the rest of my school days in this building as the school was not rebuilt until 1948–49, after I had left. It was thanks to the dedication of the teachers that most of us had exemption from matriculation, when you consider that they lost all books and equipment at a time when they were irreplaceable. We had odd desks and books from surrounding schools.

Luftwaffe tactics now included what the British termed 'tip and run' raids. These were fast, low-level daylight attacks by single or small groups of aircraft. The low-level aspect meant that the bombs travelled horizontally as they fell and were more likely to travel through walls at ground level than penetrate buildings from top to bottom. As such, casualties would have to be rescued from upper floors.

Between May 1942 and June 1943, there were seventeen such raids on Eastbourne in East Sussex. This account of the first of them was written by a local man, N. W. Hardy:

After nearly eleven months without a bomb we were beginning to forget there was a war on, or were we?

We at least were living the lives of almost normal people until suddenly, with only about ten seconds warning from the Local Alarm, the Hun swooped and once again brought death and destruction to the town. It happened at 1.52 pm.

Nine ME 109s were seen approaching Beachy Head at about 19 feet above the water. They climbed to clear the cliffs, hedge-hopped across the Downs and swooped on the town. They dropped their bombs in widely separated parts of the town – hitting St John's church and setting it on fire, scoring a direct hit on the gas works, another direct hit on the station causing severe damage to a train and station buildings. Another bomb fell on the permanent way near Cavendish Bridge and also hit a train. The Cavendish Hotel was hit, causing severe damage and trapping people under tons of debris. Three houses in Willingdon Road were wrecked by a bomb aimed at St Michael's church. Other bombs dropped in the Coal Wharf and in Commercial Road, damaging business property. The raiders also used their machine guns freely and a number of locomotives were damaged. Fishermen in a small boat were gunned as the raiders flew out to sea and one man was severely wounded. The bombs, which burst at ground level, caused considerable damage over a wide area. Although this type of attack was terrifying in its suddenness, the public kept a high standard of morale. And the defence services performed their jobs with wonderful speed and zeal ...

Casualties: five dead; thirty-six injured.

Other raids, all on East Anglian locations, are sometimes included in the Baedeker category; Lowestoft and Great Yarmouth especially were heavily bombed throughout.

The USA had come into the war following the bombing of Pearl Harbor on 7 December 1941. By the following summer, combined British and American air forces flew frequently over the East Anglian coast on their way to attack occupied Europe. Tom King was still at his ARP post in Southwold police station, just up the coast from Lowestoft. He wrote in his diary:

31st July 1942
Spent the morning in the garden and had a good sleep in the afternoon. Quiet day – a few planes. Heard on the wireless today that the Germans went to the Midlands last night and we brought down 9. Came on duty at 21.30 it was quiet up to 00.30 then our planes started to go out and it turned out to be one of the largest concentrations

Nurses take blood for testing, prior to donation, from miners in South Yorkshire. Preventing deaths during air raids through loss of blood was a key concern for medical services. New and improved methods for collecting and storing blood for transfusion had been developed during the Spanish Civil War (1936–39) by two doctors, Norman Bethune and Frederic Durán-Jordà. Dr Durán-Jordà came to Britain as a refugee from Spain and helped set up the first blood transfusion service in the UK.

ever to go over to Germany. The noise got you a bit at times, you could hardly hear oneself speak, then at 1.00 they started out from the sea and kept up until 3.45, a series of explosions that vibrated everything, doors and windows vibrated as if they would come off their hinges. And nearly all the Boro turned out, about 20 different people phoned up to ask what all the noise was about, the noise ended about 4.00 but although a hectic night, we had no sirens. Came off duty at 8.00.

At the beginning of 1943, a Focke-Wulf fighter-bomber on a 'Terror raid' dropped a high-explosive bomb on Sandhurst Road School in Catford, London. There had been no warning siren and children were sitting down to lunch when the bomb hit. Over sixty people – mostly children – were injured; thirty-eight children and six teachers were killed by the bombing.

The inquiry into the attack praised rescue services. Parents rushed to the site. Greensleeves, the official history of the WVS in the Second World War, says:

The task of taking griefstricken parents through the debris to identify whom they could among the scattered garments, satchels, bricks and glass, fell to WVS members. The heart-rending job was well done. And soon afterwards the Service was officially asked to organize Incident Inquiry Points as part of post-raid welfare. Centre organizers, District and Post Leaders were then all given appropriate training. The first WVS Incident Inquiry Point was set up after a raid in the St Pancras area during October 1943.

Also in 1943, a new device, the butterfly bomb, was dropped by the Luftwaffe for the first time. Henry Beckingham recalls:

> The two half cylinders of the casing formed a pair of wings to slow down their descent. The two end sections formed a propeller, the rotation caused the steel cable to turn and hence to turn the spindle which screwed into the fuse. When the spindle had been unscrewed approximately four turns the fuse was armed. Once armed the bomb could not be disarmed.

A large number of butterfly bombs were dropped on Britain in a raid on Grimsby and neighbouring Cleethorpes in June. Although Grimsby had endured many raids during the conflict, there had been relatively few casualties until that point. This raid resulted in ninety-nine casualties, many of them children who mistook the bombs for shrapnel and picked them up.

Joyce Pomorska, then aged 14, was at a cinema in the town:

> My father had gone out as a special constable and he didn't arrive home until very late, about ten o'clock in the morning. He told us about the bombs and that things were rather difficult and some people had been killed and he had to go out again. Well I had promised my mother to take her to see Yankee Doodle Dandy at the cinema and he warned us that we might not be able to get any transport but we did and we went to the cinema and we saw the film only to discover when we'd left that four seats away from us was a butterfly bomb. Fortunately there was no-one else in the row.

It was on the floor. I thought it was a light on the ceiling but apparently it wasn't it was a slight hole where it had come through. But nobody realised at the time what they were and practically every street was affected ...

My father took me and showed me [them] at the station. People had been bringing them in in baskets.

Well of course nobody realised that it was a dangerous thing to do and they were very fortunate that not all of them went off.

Bomb disposal teams were taking no chances. Henry Beckingham wrote afterwards:

There had been a heavy air raid on the 17th/18th August '43 in the Hull, Hedon and Hornsea areas, when a large number of butterfly bombs were dropped, causing havoc. For weeks we were still searching in the hedgerows and ditches for these lethal fragmentation bombs. In many cases we had to resort to placing straw in the ditches and setting fire to it so we could clear the thick entanglement of undergrowth.

In Wembley, Rose Uttin was still fire-watching with the Fire Guard:

September 3rd 1943
Today starts the 5th year of the war. How much longer? Last night we attended a firewatch meeting. Now we come under the new fireguard order which begins on Sept 20th. We had preliminary instructions and commence new training etc very shortly. We must have pails of water ready as our supply coming from the Colne

Valley via Watford makes us at the end of the main and should that be hit we shall be in a quandary.

Sunday 31st October 43
We had a fireguard practice this morning, one section all turned out but some did not trouble so we expect to have another practice next Sunday morning – a fine way to spend a Sunday, preparing for this …

In our exercises we had a 'bomb' in our front room and one in Mrs Bradburn's hall to put out. I rushed and got Mrs Kneebone's stirrup pump and we practised with it. A case of the nearest to hand with me. Connie Alcott ran the messages for Bill, who is the group leader and knows what to do through his City practice. One group failed to turn out so the leader had to let his 'fire' burn out and that would have meant in the real raid that the NFS would have had to have been called out.

Operation Steinbock, or the 'Little Blitz', as it was known in Britain, was launched in January 1944. The targets were mainly London and south-east England. Hermann Göring put the newly promoted General Major Dietrich Peltz in charge of the operation. He told him to avenge mass bombing of German cities by British and Allied forces.

Rose Uttin recorded the first raid of this new phase in her diary:

21 January 1944
Three years ago we were sleeping downstairs in the lounge and worrying every time we heard a plane go over. Now we go to bed and if we hear any noise listen for a moment and then go off to sleep … 8.30 pm warning

went and fires started over London. We stood at the back door until the local guns started and then came inside. It got so heavy we sat under the table – for the windows shook so I thought the glass might come in. All clear at 10.15 and so thankful we were to hear it. Raid was very bad; incendiaries etc at Wembley Park and Alperton on the Fox film studios. Vans going round telling people not to touch any bomb pieces they might find.

Sunday, 13 February
Tonight we had just finished supper, it is so dark out – I had to wait until I got used to the dark before I opened the side gate – 2 pails of water on the step. Am sitting writing this with the guns going off and my tin hat on – we are so sick of it all. Dora had gone to bed but as it got heavy about 8.45 pm she got up again. Here we all are grouped round the dining table ready to dive underneath it if anything heavy starts.

Friday, 18 February 1944
We have just passed through a nasty sharp raid, started 12.45 and all clear has just gone 1.45. It was like the Battle of Britain days. I got up at once and dressed and Bill followed.
– very heavy gunfire and incendiaries dropped in the road
– explosive ones and there was so much gunfire we did not go out for a minute but I stayed on getting water as the pails outside were frozen. Bill got the pump and went down Castelton to a house that had one incendiary through the small bedroom – the people had just got up and downstairs as it came through the roof. It

split the wardrobe and did a lot of damage but thank God no-one was hurt. Big fires in London right the way across – the red glow is still showing. How much more are we to have? 4½ years of war and we get so weary of it all. A big incendiary exploded about a minute away right by the pillar box and uprooted the tree but as it wasn't near the houses we just had to let it burn out. From the noise overhead there must have been a lot of planes. As the bombs whizzed through the air we three – Mother, Dora and I – crouched under the table, I was scared and went dry with fright.

One HE fell in the park, blowing up the children's pond – another fell in Clarendon Gardens – two houses down an old lady and gentleman still in bed were blown through the floor with the bed but got out and lost everything. 16 were killed at Blackbird Cross and lots of fires – all clear at 1.45 everywhere. Harold came in to see if we were safe as he heard it was our way.

Sunday 20th Feb
Still they come over – raid started 9.30, all clear 10.35 – not so many over us as Friday but fires are over London and lots of incendiaries fell – we just got under the table as they passed over – no sense in taking risks. We heard that Mrs Stevenson in Clarendon Gardens had two broken legs – the third house has to come down. We didn't feel so bad this time.

Monday 21st Feb
Whitehall was hit last night – Kensington and Park Royal amongst other places – Such a shock today, Mr Bradburn has passed away suddenly. He was on the gunsite at

Hampstead when it was hit and the strain was too much for him. Poor dear what she has had to put up with the last 3½ years – first her son then her husband.

24th February
Raid last night started at 10.15 – just as I had been in bed an hour – so came down and endured misery for ten minutes. This morning we went to the canteen to hear that four parashooters [parachutists] had been brought to Wembley Police Station – quiet lads, about 18. It has been funny to hear the tales that have been going round, one would think that hundreds were about. Raid started tonight at 9.40 and ended at 10.50 – terrific gunfire so we sat under the dining room table shivering and had a nip of whiskey. Many planes flying over but we didn't hear anything drop near like last Friday.

March 14th 1944
Once again I write – not of the Fire of London but Wembley. It started at 10.30 pm and the swine kept diving low till he could see he had reached his target. When Bill and I got on the step what a sight. The factories were all aflame fully 150 yards into the air – thank goodness the railway is between us and the fires – although the houses in the road must be burnt out as well. I cannot write any-more – I feel too upset as several nice girls I worked with were on night shift there. (added later: 4 factories burnt out)

For much of the United Kingdom, the Blitz was over by the spring of 1944. In Southwold, Allied planes flying to bomb Germany were a regular sight, On 22 April Tom King wrote:

Came on duty at 08.00, fairly quiet day not many planes about in the morning but several big forces of bombers in the afternoon, also fighters. No warnings during the day, came off duty at 19.00.

The police specials had an exercise tonight with the Home Guard. There is supposed to be an enemy land-ing. Crowds of planes about in the evening, they went out at 18.30. Planes returned 21.30. Beattie and myself went out to look at them, hundreds of planes were coming in and dropping red flares, made a very pretty sight but I was tired and went to bed. I'd not been there two minutes when the siren went 22.09 and heard m/c gun fire. Got up and we went outside. Saw a plane in flames to the north of the town, looked like a parachute flare going along, then it dived to ground and went up in a sheet of flame. Just before I came out another plane, a Liberator, had gone down over the town on fire and crashed at Girlings Farm Reydon in marshes near Quay Lane. Some of the crew baled out, five were found injured. One was pulled out of the sea by coastguards and Captain Clark of Coastal Battalion; the other four came down on the common and marshes. One dead airman was found at Walberswick and two were found near the plane at Reydon, so 8 were accounted for and two missing from the crew of ten. Had another plane on fire over the town, it crashed just out of our sec-tion, near Kessingland – damn. It seemed as if planes were crashing everywhere. What had happened, German planes had followed ours home and when we were dropping flares the planes made a sitting target. I heard about eight planes were shot down. One of the crew told us they never dreamt there were any enemy planes near. We had a hectic time at the Report Centre, many conflicting reports. White for red came through at 23.12, then a big force of our planes went out, and a second warning 23.21 and white 23.42, third at 00.30 and white 00.41 and 4th white 4.45. I went home to bed at 01.00 and never heard the last siren. We had no more incidents.

By 1944, Betty Bullard was stationed at HQ Transport Command in Harrow, Middlesex:

22nd February 1944
Air raids for the past five nights. It's all a little wearing. Sunday was the worst – the siren went at about 11.30 and the barrage is so noisy and things begin to shake so much that I dig out my slacks, collect a greatcoat and tin hat and go and investigate. It's all rather alarming and I am distinctly frightened: guns are terrific, incendiaries spatter down in the square, a bomb which fortunately doesn't explode whistles down on to no 17. We stand about in the hall while the fire guards rush about with buckets and cluster on the steps outside ready for a call from Mrs P who is on duty on the roof. I move a few buckets vaguely and get rather in the way. I look out of the front door to find fires all around, the post office sorting office is burnt out, so is Stewarts hotel behind Pantings. The occupants of the UXB house are evacu-ated on to us and everyone is most efficient. They are taken into the drawing room and I pour out tea for them and offer my bed to some of the poor old dears who really need it, but they refuse so I supply my eiderdown and lend an MTC girl, who incidentally knows Pam, my

dressing gown. I make myself some coffee, hot up my bottle and go to bed about 2 am.

Another raid last night. I stay in bed until I decide I'm really too frightened to stay any longer. Descend to the hall and talk to Mary and Rachel, Mrs R and a small black kitten, an orphan of the storm, and immediately feel much better.

Have offered myself as a fireguard as I feel I really ought to do something. Had to confess my ignorance of exactly what one does but they were nice about it. Nice story. Fire party ordered out to a fire, when they got there told it was too big for them, leave it for the NFS engine. Up comes 2nd fire party, unknown to 1st, rushes in and extinguishes fire. Enormous indignation of 1st party.

28th Feb 1944

More raids, in fact every night until Saturday. Lots of fires on Wed. Went on the roof with Mary after the all-clear and could feel the heat of a house up the road where the top floors were blazing and the roof had fallen in. NFS got it under control very efficiently all in about 20 minutes. Miss Pepper and fire party distinguished themselves, they were called out to one fire, then on to another; two men overcome by smoke so they pulled them out, kept it under control till the NFS arrived and just got out before the roof caved in. NFS congratulated them and presented Miss P with the bomb. American soldier 'I think you ladies are wonderful, may I shake you by the hand?'

'Scalded Cat' raids were a relatively late feature of aerial warfare. These were short, sharp, high-level raids in which a few fast planes would drop their bombs and quickly head off before anti-aircraft guns and civil defence sirens could swing into action.

In Eastbourne, N.W. Hardy recorded the first such raids over the town, in March 1944:

March 14th

Three hostile planes of the fighter bomber type crossed the coast near Langley Point in moonlight with engines shut off. They glided over the town, released their bombs, restarted their engines and headed for home. One bomb hit the station and severely damaged numbers 2 and 3 tracks and the station buildings. A second bomb exploded in Hartfield Square, severely damaging house property and setting fire to a number of Army trucks, jeeps and motor cycles. The third dropped in the sea off Langley Point.

Casualties: one slightly injured.

V-1S AND V-2S

The Little Blitz ended in May 1944. It had been a failure for the Luftwaffe even though it had committed large numbers of planes to the attacks. One reason was that the UK's ground and air defences were far better developed than they had been at the start of the war. The campaign had taken aircrew and aircraft from other operations and the Luftwaffe did not recover its strength to fight the Allied invasion of Europe, which began the following month. The Little Blitz was the last offensive bombing campaign by the Luftwaffe in the Second World War.

In the UK, though, this was not the end of aerial attacks. New weapons, known as V-1s, launched from sites along the French and Dutch coasts, took up the attack.

The V-1 was a pilotless plane powered by a simple jet engine. It travelled at speeds of up to 350 miles an hour. When it reached a preset location, in all but the latest models, the engine would cut out and it would go into a dive. A few seconds later it would hit the ground and the warhead

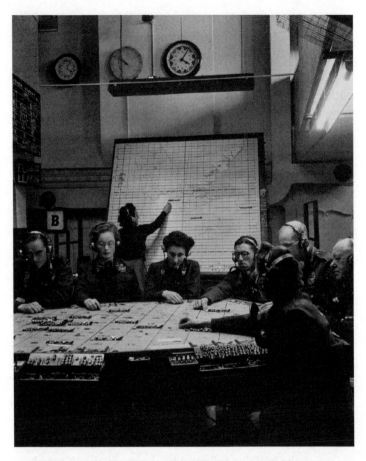

The Bromley Centre of the Royal Observer Corps in October 1943. Initially a civilian volunteer force, the Observer Corps was formed in 1925. It was the only means of tracking enemy aircraft once they had passed over the British coastline. They warned of enemy aircraft approaching so that sirens could be sounded, and became the Royal Observer Corps in 1941 in recognition of their contribution during the Battle of Britain. That same year their numbers were increased greatly, mainly by the introduction of women of the Women's Auxiliary Air Force. *Courtesy of Imperial War Museum*

would explode. People soon recognised the low pulse of the engine, which gave rise to the nickname 'buzz-bomb'. It was also known commonly as the 'fly-bomb' or 'doodlebug'. V-1s could be launched at any time of the day or night and, initially, anti-aircraft measures were ineffective against them. Soon 100 V-1s were being launched each day at London and many towns and cities within the weapon's 200-mile range.

The first V-1s fell on London on 13 June 1944. Shortly after, Kenneth Holmes, a teenager living in north London, started recording his thoughts:

28.6.1944

I have decided to write this diary after 13 days of almost incessant air attacks on London by Hitler's much vaunted 'Secret Weapon' the 'Flying Bomb', since named by the public 'buzz bombs' and 'pilotless planes', later officially termed by the German High Command as V1s.

I will always remember the 20th June our fifth day of flying bombs. I was in the GPO in Tottenham Court Rd. when I heard a rumbling in the distance which sounded familiar as by this time I was becoming accustomed to the sound of flying bombs. But as the alert had not sounded I decided to ignore it. At that moment the bell rang in the building followed by the sirens, the PO clerk said there was 'imminent danger and they were closing' (and she wasn't joking). I strolled across the road to my employment and had just got inside the building when there was a tremendous explosion which shook the entire building and threw me across the floor a matter of six or seven yards. I picked myself up and found the room full of dust as though a terrific gust of wind had blown in. I thought my last hour had come. I went out into the street and saw a great pall of smoke rising further down the road, and decided to investigate. But what I saw I will always remember. The scene was indescribable, the bomb had crashed about 80yds away actually at the rear of Tottenham Court Rd police station, which is always thronged with people, they were wandering about in a dazed condition faces streaming with blood. Mothers with bandaged hands, legs and feet, covered all over in dust. A horse lay dead, a victim of the surprise attack, shop windows completely blown out and shattered huge lumps of masonry some smeared with blood, and glass scattered everywhere, ambulances speeding in both directions, civil defence workers already searching for victims. Civil and military police including American moving the sightseers onwards, American soldiers were even helping the rescuers in their work which gained the admiration of all onlookers, including myself. Many lives must have been saved by this prompt action of the authorities and the speed with which they worked in typical London fashion of getting on with the job, as I was on the scene within 3 minutes and found the various organisation, military, CD and police all busily engaged. And even our great American ally seemed to welcome the opportunity of being able to render assistance. I thanked God I was safe and uninjured, though a little shaken. The average Londoner took it well though many said they would prefer the Blitz bombs to these weapons. I believe people are beginning to see that it is going to be longer than they had anticipated.

V-1s were also a common sight on the Suffolk coast, as Tom King noted:

1st July

I was doing a little gardening in the evening about 19.40 when I heard a noise like a traction engine from a plane. At once thought it was a Fly Bomb. Out at sea I could see a small plane going along at about 200ft up and flying north. I went to RC and phoned through to the coast-guards to ask if it was one, they said they did not know. At 19.50 we had a red through with white 20.00. We then had a report from coastguards that it was a Fly Bomb and it landed in the sea east of Kessingland. I never heard an explosion, I don't believe there was one. This is the first Fly bomb we have had pass the town. I hope we don't get any more.

A few weeks later, Hetty Long, a widow living in Camberley, Surrey, wrote about the attacks to a friend:

Horsham Sussex

July 25th 1944

I have thought about you and your friend and feared that those dreadful things would pass your way, and one can only pray to God to protect all dear friends from danger. We get many alerts and some nights are very disturb-ing, the nearest crash 2 miles away, 3 in the night, the floor shook.

On June 15th I arranged to spend the night in London with my only sister, she lives at Streatham, which had had much damage. We went to bed about 11 pm and at 11.45 pm the first plane passed over, an awful noise from the engine, we got up at once, then the alert went and before we left the room, the explosion. We went down-stairs quickly to the Morrison shelter, and remained all

night. It was a dreadful night. The guns sounded as tho'
they were right over our heads, on the roof. About 3 am
one passed very low over the house and almost before
we could speak we heard the explosion. I thought it had
hit my sister's house and really looked for it to collapse,
but it had gone over the next row of houses and crashed
on a house straight across from my sister's back bedroom
windows, killed all the occupants, hundreds of windows
broken, but in her house no damage, the doors and windows blew open. She had a good deal of damage in 1940,
but it is a well-built house in the residential part. With
my nerves not very good after the long strain of nursing my husband, I really was terrified, tho' she remained
very calm, and so worried on my account, she thought
I would collapse. The alert was on until 10 am and the
noise going on all night. It was the first night those horrible doodlebugs came over and I shall always remember
it, and the alerts went on all the morning. I left on the
6.34 pm train, feeling such a coward to leave my sister
alone. She is a widow, [and] I begged her to come here,
but she said if she left her house she would go where
there were no alerts. The nights became worse, and to
my great relief she left London on June 20th to join her
daughter and little granddaughter at Combe Martin. Her
daughter has taken a flat there for the duration and I
hope my sister will remain there. I have a mattress under
the stairs, and when daylight comes, go up to my bed
to rest; and sleep if possible. I feel so thankful that my
dear husband has been spared this terrible time, greatly
as I feel my loss, but my anxiety with his helplessness
was almost beyond endurance when enemy planes were
above us. These are indeed terrible days, and I do feel so

sorry you have so many around you, and I am so thankful
you are both safe. I have been alone all the time, as I feel
no one would care to come to a danger zone.

Jeanne and Marion Thompson were 13-year-old twin
sisters living in north-west London. They recalled later:

Of course, at that time, we were not allowed to venture
far from home except to go to school and back, so when
the summer holidays of 1944 began and six empty weeks
stretched ahead of us, we decided to make up all sorts of
games to play and keep ourselves entertained. One of these
was tracking the flying bombs as they came over our house
and recording them in a log book. We divided the day into
fifteen-minute periods of 'watch', each sister taking her
turn to listen out for a doodlebug and writing it in the log.

On July 21st 1944, the first day of the school holidays,
we took up our positions diligently, ears pricked and
pen in hand. Between 8.15 and 1.30 pm we recorded 30
but we had no time at all to note the thirty-first for, as it
passed above the house, the engine cut out and we knew
it was about to come down. Our mother, who was in the
kitchen nearby, ran in and grabbed us and we piled into
the small cupboard under the stairs. As the bomb hurtled
to the ground, the noise was deafening, like the rushing
of an express train, ending with a huge bang. At the time,
we were sitting on top of a lot of bottled fruit which had
been stored for the winter and all the lids of the jars flew
off, covering us in bits of fruit and juice. The cupboard
door jammed and we had to force it open. When we
managed to get out into the hall, a scene of devastation
met our eyes. The front door of the house was halfway up

the stairs and there was dust, glass, smashed furniture and ornaments everywhere. Although our house had not been directly hit (the one opposite was totally destroyed), it was very badly damaged and not liveable in, so, after a night at a local rest centre, we left for our grandmother's home in the north of England where we stayed until April 1945.

V–1s reached Wembley, where Rose Uttin was still on duty:

August 13th 1944 Sunday
Up to and including tonight – 56 nights of fire watch for us all in turn, a longer spasm than the Battle of Britain. We did have six weeks and then a lull but now the warning goes without fail every night at 11 pm … we fireguards sleep in all our clothes at night except our shoes and top coats in order to be out of the house in the least possible time – it is two months now since we completely undressed to go to bed. After four years of being a fireguard we have been issued with navy armlets with the words 'Fireguard' printed on them in white – so far we haven't needed them. It is now 11.30 and I am going up to lie on the bed and get a little rest. Talk about turning night into day.

August 29th
Another day of buzz bombs. Mrs Cooper and I went to the canteen morning and afternoon (WVS). Just as we were walking along the road the klaxon went and a neighbour dragged us in to take shelter. It struck me as rather funny to get under a shelter in midday and I felt like giggling, so did Mrs Cooper. We stopped long enough to hear it drop – and then politely thanked her and went off again.

Measures to combat V-1s directly included anti-aircraft batteries, barrage balloons and fighter aircraft. Tracking the V-1s presented new challenges for the Royal Observer Corps. Eric Wilton, at the ROC Centre in Bromley, Kent, explained:

On the long-range board a cluster of red-dotted plaques fringing the coast of Kent shows that we shall not have long to wait before the next wave of raiders comes in. Jerry loves to time his attacks to a schedule and you can normally bank on a good big salvo somewhere around 11 o'clock. These plaques indicate radar plots. Somewhere in the gathering darkness of the English Channel nine evil shapes are streaking low across the calm water; and in a hundred operations rooms, on aerodromes and gunsites and in Observer Corps Centres, by this miracle of science, their courses are being accurately charted and plans laid in good time for their destruction. Already the fighter patrols that constitute the first line of defence are taking their toll. A plotter takes down a plaque from the long-range board and calls to the Duty Controller above: 'Diver 101 removed'.

Now the first plaque has moved inland. Maidstone's posts have picked up the tell-tale light from the flaming propulsion duct. From now on it's up to the Observer Corps …

It takes the doodle bug no time at all to cover the few short miles between the coast and Bromley's boundary …

Diver 104 seems to be coming our way. Roger 0373. Queenie 8985. That line will bring him bang over the centre. Already the heavy throb of his propulsion unit, with its curious overtone of urgency, can be heard clearly above the noises of the room. Queenie eight seven eight five: the noise is deafening now. There is only one thought in the room, though no one betrays it; suppose he cuts ... Some day if this goes on, one is bound to cut at the right, the unlucky place ... the walls vibrate. The air in the room seems to throb. He must be terribly low. Sometimes they don't cut. Sometimes they just dive headlong with the engine racing ...

This was not after all, the one ...

While Diver 104 has been monopolising so much of our attention three other flying bombs have been moving across other parts of the table, and a fourth, caught in the vast balloon barrage some six miles south of Bromley, has exploded in mid-air. Within a few minutes, all these raids have run their course. Out of nine indicated by radar, five have reached the table. The other four presumably have been shot down by guns or fighters on the strongly defended coastal belt. Four out of nine, plus one caught by the balloons: not a bad bag! Week by week the number of radar plots that do not reach the Bromley table is creeping up.

In Islington, London, teenager Harry Atterbury, was having a lie-in:

On a quiet Sunday morning after a warning had sounded and after I had promised to leave my bed to follow my parents who had left the house to take shelter in the brick street shelters, a V1 crashed at the corner of the street about 200 feet away. My parents' home was completely demolished with me underneath. I was still alive because my bedroom door had been blown inwards, twisted in

the air and had somehow fallen over the bed, resting on
the top and bottom bed frames, creating a space in which
I was saved from being crushed. The door held the debris
off me. I soon regained consciousness, choked with the
soot, dust and smoke; terrified by the noise, shouts and
screaming. My reaction was to struggle and shout until I
suddenly noticed a chink of light to one side above me
through which I eventually pushed my hand. This action
led to a frantic effort to get to me by some rescue workers who had seen the movement and I was pulled out
quite naked and bleeding from the numerous abrasions
caused mostly by flying glass and scratches from jagged
wood. I had a coat or blanket put round me and was
carefully carried in the arms of one of the rescuers, up
and over the debris of my home.

At the same time I saw my mother and father framed
by what was left of the front door jambs, standing crying
and in a state of shock, hardly believing that they could
see and hear me again. After they had been assured that I
was not seriously hurt, we were led through the smoking
rubble and past so many people tearing at and digging
into the ruins of other houses, where other people were
still buried.

Whether it was reality or not, I still remember seeing
the head of an old lady who had lived next door lying on
top of the ruins of her home and I believe detached from
her body. Another horror came when after a few yards
we stopped, whilst a couple of the rescuers removed the
boots from two legs that were protruding from the chaos
of broken bricks with the intention of putting them
on me. At that time I did not know that the legs were
artificial and belonged to a man who had still not been

rescued; knowledge of that would not have made the situation or nightmare any easier for me.

We were led to the underground station at Essex Road where there was some emergency help offered. Word was sent to my sisters, who were living at Stoke Newington, and we were soon collected by them. We went to the home of my sister, Ada, in Hackney. Over the next few weeks I returned to dig in the debris of our home although there was little left to recover. But on one occasion, two/three weeks later, when raising up the corner of our flattened kitchen table, I was startled and horrified when a filthy, stinking lump of fur moved and I took into my hands our old pet cat still alive. On the bus to Stoke Newington so many other passengers expressed sympathy for her, even in that filthy state. She lived with us for several years after, until the day she was killed by a car.

During those days, my older brother, Alfred, was rescued from drowning when the landing craft on which he served as a gunner was sunk during the Normandy landings. He was not informed about the V1 that destroyed our home and only discovered this later when, after hospitalization, he was allowed home on sick leave. When he emerged from the underground station at Essex Road, he witnessed the sight of flattened and destroyed streets where his home had once been. One shock on top of another weakened his health so he never regained his vigour; this resulted in his early death just five years after the war's end.

The V-1 had to be launched from a long ramp. These ramps were easily spotted from the air, making them easy targets for RAF bombers. At a press conference at the Ministry of Information on Thursday, 7 September 1944, Duncan Sandys MP, chairman of the Flying-Bomb Counter-Measures Committee, told the media that, 'Except possibly for a few last parting shots, what has come to be known as the Battle for London is over.'

He added that, during eighty days' bombardment, 8,000 bombs had been launched. Of those, 2,300 had reached the London area, where 92 per cent of all fatalities from V-1s occurred:

> This form of attack can be carried on from air bases right in the heart of Germany, if necessary. I think that in the next few weeks, Germany will have other things to think about, but from the operational point of view there is no reason whatever why these airborne launches should not be based on airfields inside Germany. For that reason we cannot assure the public categorically that flying bomb attacks have ceased once and for all but we can feel reasonably confident that the launching of any big-scale attack will be very remote indeed.

He was being over-optimistic: the following evening, at about 6.40 p.m., people in west London heard what sounded like a clap of thunder. The first V-2 had fallen at Chiswick, killing three people and seriously injuring ten. Within seconds another had fallen at Epping, causing little damage.

V-2s were rockets that travelled faster than the speed of sound – so fast that it was impossible to warn of their coming.

The Government was very worried at the public's reaction to attacks by weapons against which there was no defence and would not admit to the reality of the new weapons. Instead, official sources said that the loud noise and widespread devastation were caused by exploding gas mains. Soon people were cynically referring to the rockets as 'flying gas mains'.

During the next six months, over 1,000 V-2 rockets and nearly 500 V-1 flying bombs landed across the United Kingdom.

Kenneth Holmes was interested in the official silence over the new weapons he saw and heard around him:

Friday 8.9.44

As I was writing my diary tonight at 6.45 pm there was a colossal explosion (certainly the loudest I had heard) which rocked the entire house and shook the windows violently, followed by a rumbling for a few seconds, and then a softer explosion. I at once thought that Hitler's threatened 'rocket bombardment' had begun but no other explosions followed. I tried to get the idea from my head then I thought it couldn't have been a doodlebug because there were no sirens sounded and besides a flying bomb doesn't make an explosion as loud as that, I also doubted if it was a pick-a-back plane [some V-1s were launched from planes in mid-air] because of the fact that there was no alert. Well what else could it be? More like a gasometer had exploded or maybe a munitions dump? I tried to think it was one of these but all the time at the back of my mind there was a doubt as I asked myself is this the beginning of a new bombardment for London by long-range rockets? However time will tell!

Thursday 14.9.44

I was awakened this morning at 5 am by two more shattering explosions, both the explosions shook the house and rattled the windows. I was told later that the explosions (which I think are the enemies' long-range rocket shells) occurred at Walthamstow E and Dagenham, Essex again. I have been looking in every paper to see if there was any mention of these 'explosions' but there is nothing at all. Why are we not being told about these? Obviously security measures which convinces me that they must be rockets.

Betty Bullard's brother, Dr Edward Bullard, was Scientific Adviser to the Air Ministry and the Admiralty. As her diary shows, lack of information about the V-2s did nothing to stifle discussion among the wider public:

15th September 1944

Teddy is advising Air Marshal Hill at ADGB [Air Defence Great Britain] on the rocket bombs that are arriving from Holland. They weigh 16 tons and travel faster than sound, go 55 miles up into the air and down again and cost £40,000 each! However, there's only one ton of explosives and not many have come over yet.

Morrison [Herbert Morrison, Minister for Home Security] of course has not allowed anything to be given out to the papers yet and everyone is talking about mysterious bangs and 'gas mains' blowing up. 4 more doodle bombs [V-1s] this morning launched from a/c [aircraft] over the N[orth] sea.

A Food Flying Squad mobile canteen. Such canteens, usually run by WVS volunteers, took refreshment to rescue workers, fire-fighters and victims at bomb sites.

Kenneth Holmes continues:

Thursday 5.10.44
More flying bombs were launched against London and
southern England during the early hours of this morning causing damage and casualties. An alert sounded this
evening at 8 pm lasting about 30 minutes and there were
two explosions in the distance. These headlines appeared
in today's Daily Mail:

'Germans decide V2 has failed', 'Dutch-based weapon too
inaccurate', 'Atom bombs to be speeded up' (by the enemy).

The *Daily Mail* reports were by Ralph Hearns, the newspaper's correspondent in Stockholm.

Thursday 26.10.44
There were two tremendous explosions early this morning
followed as usual by the rumbling sound as if buildings are
crumbling down – after the explosion. Security measures
are very strict apparently as the public are not encouraged
to refer to these explosions as rockets but are still being
talked about as 'gas main explosions', which of course
seems absurd, though obviously to prevent the enemy
from knowing where these have actually landed. One of
these landed near London Bridge railway station and the
other at Clapham Junction. There is still no mention of
these 'mysterious explosions' in either press or radio.

By now, Mollie Wilson was stationed at Elstree in
Hertfordshire, in a large house with several other WAAFs,
where she experienced her first V-2:

Crash! Our greenhouse collapsed, our windows shattered. The duty officer flew up the stairs with her Red Cross box and someone put the kettle on for a late brew. Then suddenly, out of the blue, came a roar, a flash, and a second explosion, bigger and more terrifying, lighting up the sky. That was the very first V2 rocket. It gave you no warning at all. By the time you heard it, it was too late to worry. After a while we got used to these, too.

Meanwhile in Becton, east London, Betty Holbrook, an ATS radar operator in Anti-Aircraft, was being briefed:

One day all the Radar Operators were called together for a meeting. Something new was in the air. V2s had become a menace and the latest idea was to try and find out at what angles they came down and to fire in those directions and so explode them in the air. Normally, the Receiver was rotated in its search for targets, as only when directly facing a target could it pick up a signal.

Now we were to do a 'watch' every night from 7 pm to 8.30 am, and for this purpose both the Transmitter and the Receiver would be lashed to a certain bearing, so that if any target were seen on the tubes, it would be coming in on that bearing; and directly at us!

I was on the first watch with Joy and Joan. We went into the Receiver at 10 pm and stayed there until 7.30 am when we were relieved for breakfast. For this operation we did not need transmitter operators. Joan (our number one) wore headphones with a tannoy fitment. She had a stopwatch and a pad of forms to fill in. Every half hour a voice would come through the headphones. 'Synchronise

stop watches! Five … eight, nine, ten and the time is …!'
and Joan checked her stopwatch.

We then sat and waited, sometimes talking, sometimes
just sitting – but never sleeping. It was very difficult to
stay awake.

But it was most important to stay awake, because
when we had to move we had to move FAST! As soon
as a V2 was launched from its site across the channel, Joan
received a command, 'Big Ben! Big Ben! Big Ben!'

She repeated this to us. We then operated certain
switches etc according to a specified 'drill'. We gazed stead-
ily at the illuminated tube waiting for a target to appear. We
knew that the target would be moving at a fantastic speed.
As soon as the V2 crossed the coast of England we got
the command, 'Alarm! Alarm! Alarm!' We watched even
closer. It was not often that we did see anything, which did
not bother us at all as we were very conscious of the fact
that when we did, the 'thing' was coming straight for us!!

While we were gazing at the tubes, Joan would be
receiving, 'Five … eight, nine, TEN!' So when there was
something on the screen we had to record Bearings and
Angles every five seconds. We called these out to Joan,
who recorded them on a special form which was taken
to London by a despatch rider early the next morning.

In Southwold ARP Tom King recorded the damage from
the continuing V-1 (Fly) attacks in the town and beyond:

14th Oct
Had a warning at 19.53 when I was on duty, it was fairly
quiet at first and then all the guns opened up on a Fly. I
looked outside, just as I got there a shell hit on the Fly,

there was a terrific flash of orange flame followed by a hell of an explosion, glass fell everywhere about 300 houses, 57 shops, the church and two chapels were damaged, fortunately only one person, a soldier, was slightly hurt by shrapnel. We had a busy time at RC [Report Centre] there is a hell of a mess in the town. It was good shooting by the heavy and light AA [Anti-Aircraft]. I believe it was the light that got it down.

6th November

At 20.16 we had a warning; 8 Fly Bombs went past the town and six were shot down by gunfire. I saw 5 of them explode. They were all south and just out of our area. The searchlight at Easton came up several times, one Fly crashed on landing in the Minsmere area after having its tail shot off, white 21.01. Crowds of our planes came back at 21.30 and the guns opened up on one of them but missed thank God.

As Kenneth Holmes' diary shows, V-2s became a terrifying part of daily life:

Sunday 5.11.44

Today I witnessed the nearest escape I have had so far, once again I thanked God that my family and myself were untouched though a little shaken. This morning very early there was another 'tremendous explosion' and yet another at 10.15 am. It was about 5.15 pm and I was slowly strolling down the road passing a street shelter when I saw a vivid flash just above me. Thinking it was lightning, as it was raining I took no notice but immediately after there was a tremendous explosion followed by the sound of breaking glass. I at once threw myself against the shelter (or was I blown?) and covered my neck and face the best I could with my hands. At that moment I thought the end of the world had come. The earth trembled, the very air seemed to vibrate, my ears seemed to be deafened, and a buzzing sound was passing through them. I cannot adequately describe my feelings. I thought I was accustomed to hearing 'bangs' and 'explosions' but never have I heard such a deafening sound and it is surprising what one's ears can receive and remain normal. I didn't need telling the cause of this explosion and as it was the 5th of November, I realised instantly that this was one of Hitler's 'fireworks', be it a rocket V2, V3 or whatever else the German High Command name them. I was only a few yards from my home but I covered the distance in record time to see if my family were safe. I found my Mother and Father quite safe and Dad busy inspecting the damage and though no words were said to the effect, I sensed by the look on my mother's face, her relief that I too was safe. The table was laid for tea, which of course, now would have to wait because the important job at the moment (to Dad at least) was to get the damage patched up temporarily and quickly before blackout time, which would be in about half an hour's time. The window frame had been blown into the room and here I would again remind you that the frame contains a white canvas substituting glass. Of the few remaining windows at the back of the house 6 were shattered, the locks had again been blown off from the doors, and though all this was most annoying, on a 'quiet Sunday afternoon' my innermost thoughts were for the more unfortunate victims (not far away), maybe killed, maimed or suffering untold agony under the debris of what was, a few moments ago, their homes, which gave me a feeling of thankfulness that at least we were spared. Here I must confess my youthful curiosity urged me to investigate. I didn't have to travel far, as 100yds away in a thickly populated area, ambulances were already on the scene and treating casualties. I saw several people suffering from cuts and bleeding, waiting to be treated (a miniature battlefield), houses I had known well were just not there, and the debris appeared to be around the surrounding houses (what was left of those). Goodness knows where the houses that had been struck had disappeared to! It looked as though a huge bulldozer had lifted them from the earth and there was quite an open space. Other houses in the immediate vicinity were badly blasted and partly demolished, a sight with which I have become familiar, but never have I seen houses or buildings so cleanly swept away as I have already described, and here note most of these are 3 and 4 storey tenement houses sheltering 3, 4 and even 5 families. Surrounding streets over an area of ½ a mile (including my own) suffered damage, shop windows were shattered and their goods lying on the pavement. I also noticed large pieces of clay scattered even as far as 300yds from the 'incident' which told me the missile must have struck very deep and to add to all this a heavy downpour, which must have hampered the rescuers. This is certainly the worst 'incident' I have experienced and I feel sure the casualties will be heavy. During the day we had three rockets.

Monday 6.11.44

More flying bombs were launched last night, a few fell over a scattered area and minor incidents were reported at a number of places. Today there have been no explosions, at least none that I have heard. Digging is still going on (all day) today for people trapped in the incident yesterday (Boothby Rd, St John's Way N19). It has been continuing all through the night and today even as I write (9.30 pm) the rescuers are working with the aid of searchlights. I have been told that in the house the rocket crashed on, there was a children's party in progress and there are said to have been between 25–30 young children at the party. Also two Alsatian dogs trained especially to scent and discover persons trapped have been brought in, these dogs have been used in many flying bomb incidents. I'm afraid the casualty list will be heavy because this is a busy junction and shopping centre where people queue for buses and these would most certainly become casualties. Had this happened on a Saturday it would have been more disastrous as the centre is a very well-known shopping area, also the traffic is more busy then. There was also a bus and a tram blasted. Walking past the scene of the 'incident' today it indeed looks like a battlefield; glass is scattered everywhere, the fronts of shops blown in, shutters twisted and buckled, ambulances and police cars parked and many sightseers. It is indeed a terrible sight. I said a week or two ago that I hoped I would never get a chance to judge which caused more damage, a flying bomb incident or a rocket, now I have had my opportunity, from this incident and what I have seen, I personally think a rocket. During the day we had one alert.

Tuesday 7.11.44
Rescue work is still carrying on in Boothby Road N19 day and night. I have been told the search is being made for the children as only a few have been found.

Wednesday 8.11.44

I noticed today that the rescue workers had ceased in Boothby Rd N19 apparently late last night. People in the district say that not all the victims were rescued and many still lay dead beneath the ruins, some of course were even blown to pieces and will never be recovered. This does not make very pleasant reading but they are plain facts which should be placed on 'Germany's account'. I am sure the rescue workers did everything in their power to find the buried and deserve the best of praise. I am told the casualty list is 43 killed, 83 hospital cases, and a 100-odd walking wounded, which makes a total of 226 innocent civilians. I realise more than ever now that we are indeed very fortunate to be alive through God's mercy and had this particular rocket crashed a little nearer – this page would never have been written!

Today there has been the first mention of the V2 in the press – after two months of these 'mysterious explosions'. This is what I read: Berlin – 'V2 attack on Greater London Begun', 'Speed 1,000mph says neutral'.

'The German High Command announced this afternoon that V2 attacks on London had begun. In their daily communiqué they said "the area of Greater London has been under fire since June 15 with short interruptions and in varying strength … The fire has been intensified for some weeks past by the use of a second and far more effective missile the V2."'

Betty Holbrook survived a V-2 attack on Becton:

I was walking from the Transmitter to the Manning Hut, deep in thought, when, suddenly I found myself being rushed backwards, absolutely unable to help myself. The air around and above me was vibrating madly. I was horribly frightened. I was nearly back to where the Transmitter stood and was wondering what was going to happen when the TX and myself meet. There was a tremendous explosion and pieces came down out of the sky. I saw everything as through a rippling pool of water. For a second everything was quiet. The TX door opened and two came out, looking as amazed as I felt. We looked at one another and said together, 'Yes, it WAS!' And pretended to wipe perspiration from our brows. Pretended?!! That was a V2 exploding in the air. Just a few yards from where I had been standing, I found a big wheel-like thing full of marble-sized ball bearings. It was heavy: this was part of a V2. It was well and truly embedded in the ground. I was just a little shaken. But picked it up to keep as a souvenir, forever!

After that episode we never went around alone, always there were at least two together. This feeling of not wanting to die alone was very, very strong. Personally, my greatest horror was that of having one moment of intense fear; that of actually seeing a V2 or FB [flying bomb] sitting beside me for one part of a second before it exploded. This, I was sure, I could not survive!!

Anti-aircraft measures and the capture of launch sites by British and Allied forces curtailed V-1 and V-2 attacks, but they continued to bring death and destruction across the country right up until the end of the war.

9

CLEARING UP

After the failure of Operation Steinbock, the Luftwaffe was no longer a threat and the blackout no use against V-1s and V-2s. From September 1944, civil defence services were wound down. The blackout was replaced by the dim-out, except for a 5-mile strip along the coastline of the UK, where it continued.

J. Grenville Atherton's diary records celebrations for the dim-out in Manchester:

September 1944 was a 'black-out breakthrough' as the lights were switched on again at night in Manchester and Salford. Various towns had consultations with the Town Clerk (Mr J.W. Trewas in Stretford), the Chief Constable, and 'Lighting Superintendent' (grand title). On Tuesday 12th September, 1944 I joined hundreds of sightseers in Manchester to see the street lamps lit. The Manchester Evening News printed photographs with the caption: 'the illuminations in St Peter's Square caused gasps of

Long after the bombers had gone, long after the war ended, bomb disposal
squads were still busy dealing with unexploded bombs (UXBs). Here,
in 1949, a squad is removing a large warhead from a bomb or landmine,
originally dropped in 1940.

amazement.' For once the reporters got it right. There were shrieks of excitement and more than one person was seen striking matches just for the novelty. How different everywhere looked.

Mollie Wilson wrote to her parents about a trip to London with a boyfriend, John, on the last days of his leave from the RAF:

20th September 1944
Generally, the dim-out has not been a great success but Boreham Wood has not managed too badly. In particular, I noticed a block of flats, with each floor a complete tier of light. They had, by accident or design – all their windows covered with orange curtains, a colour which certainly enhances the brightness of electricity in nights as dark as these we have now. It was like a fairyland after all these years, and I was completely fascinated. Some people, of course, do not bother with the new relaxation, because if a warning sounded, there is such a terrific flap – and, as you will have heard on the wireless, we do still have an occasional siren. Instead of shrugging their shoulders and carrying on reading or darning socks or whatever they've been doing, they have to trip about in the dark, struggling with shutters and things they can't see. No wonder they are none too enthusiastic, but believe me, if they knew how good the lights make all us homeless people feel, they'd endure even that ...

Walking along in central London ... along the Thames Embankment. Eventually, just as it was getting dark, we disembarked at Charing Cross, and walked all the way along the Embankment, eating apples and flinging

the cores into the Thames. You know, I have been terribly lucky. Always, I have dreamed of doing just these
things, and there was little reason why my dreams should
have come true. There are so many air force stations in
England, and so many away from London. And yet we
strolled along as though it was the most natural thing
in the world. Silly, isn't it? We sat on a bench under the
trees, watching light flickering on the opposite bank, and
buses running across the bridges and either side of us.
Everything was rather dimmed and muted by a soft, fine
mist and London was very quiet. Trams passing behind us
flashed lights on our faces and policemen passed swing-
ing their batons. It was all so wonderful I could have
stayed there all night – though it would not have been
very seemly. We listened to Big Ben striking 8, 8.15, 8.30,
8.45 and nine, and just as I began to think I ought to
be moving, what do you suppose? In a house behind us
on the opposite side of the street, someone struck up
Tchaikovsky's Piano Concerto. Remember the one I
love so much … At about 9.20, we started back as I had
come on night duty – and that was that. In a little while
he'll be ringing me to say 'Goodbye' and I shall take up
my visits to the Landergains or resume my dancing again,
as though he'd never been.

Betty Bullard was not impressed. She wrote in her diary:

22nd September 1944
The Dim Out is disappointing as practically none of the
street lamps are working and everywhere is practically
pitch black and grim. Got to have some kind of curtain
and the only thing most people have is blackout. However

I don't put up the shutters now except of course when the siren sounds, which it has done tonight.

For Rose Uttin, life was improving:

Monday Sept 11 1944
At last we are free from firewatching. The idea of going to bed every night without the thought of possible raids is wonderful to contemplate. Saturday the word comes through that firewatching is finished. It is four years since Mrs Bradburn and I kept watch on the steps – and I never thought it would last so long.

But the raids continued:

Sept 30th
Raids and doodlebugs on and off since I last wrote (11th Sept). Went to Winnie's yesterday and two warnings as soon as we got in. Another at 4.45 up and down, we are more than sick of it – war no nearer to being over than this time last year.

Throughout the war there were clear divisions of opinion in Britain among those who experienced air raids regarding the bombing of German civilians. V.M.H. Owen, leading Wren coder at Fort Southwick, wrote to her parents:

July 9th 1944
I have just been talking to another Wren about bombing – I don't know how it cropped up but she said she sympathised with the newspaper campaign in favour of our bombing Germany indiscriminately until they stop

the flying bomb – in fact she thinks of bombing them to revenge their bombing us – don't you think that attitude is wrong – that it would be as much a confession on our side of failure and that we can't take the bombing, as it is on their side. Besides I don't think it would help shorten the war and would only do ourselves far more harm after the war that we lowered ourselves to their level – same as I still think it is a mistake for us to have shackled the prisoners to retaliate for their shackling ours – though I entirely see the point of view – but of course I have very little right to talk about it – never having seen a bomb in my life – but don't you agree with me?

Rose Uttin was of a different opinion:

Nov 9th 1944
The second warning had just gone at 10.15 and we sit waiting. I feel somehow I could not bear to scramble under the table tonight and it is so cold the shelter would be intolerable. As I feel at the moment I loathe and despise anything to do with the war and I am sick of thinking how we must 'sit back and take it'. Mr Churchill said that at the Mansion House today 'we must exert every ounce of energy tired as we are after more than five years of war' – tired is mild to what we really feel and we have to do 'the nice thing' for posterity's sake and the history books that will be written about it. Personally I don't care a dam what the historians write – for the fifth generation to follow – if they have any sense they will start their wars good and proper without observing any of the niceties that our government are doing now – in case they offend the Germans. I spoke to one woman in

Lyons yesterday – her husband has been abroad with the troops five years and she was sick of everything.

In 1945 Kenneth Holmes, read about the last RAF bombs to fall on Berlin, commented:

> We living in Southern England cannot help but feel pity for the Berliners when we hear that 'our bombers were out over Berlin again last night.'

Constance Logan-Wright was a member of the London executive of Bundles for Britain Inc., a US initiative that provided essential items to people who had been bombed out. This report followed her visit to those sheltering in caves in Dover – many of whom, as the war ended, had no other place to live:

> 16th November 1944
> Thinking that Bundles members might be interested in first hand news of Britain's front line town – Dover – Lady Beatty and I went down there for the day last week. During the five years of war the population had dropped from 42,000 to 14,500. Many people had left soon after the outbreak of war but very many others did not leave till their homes were destroyed or made uninhabitable by shelling ...

After lunch:

> We then drove on to the largest of Dover's cave shelters. With 100 feet of sheer cliff towering over it, it gave its shelterers a wonderful sense of security and these caves

have literally saved many hundreds of lives. The entrance
is in space quarried out of the cliff-face in the days of the
great sailing ships. These ships, having discharged their
cargoes, were in need of ballast and the easily quarried
limestone 'of the white cliffs' proved very useful. On
the outbreak of the present war, the tunnelled cliff face
was hurriedly extended into great long galleries radiat-
ing from a kind of central hall, and into these galleries
were put three-tier sleeping bunks. The shelter we saw
could accommodate 2,300 men, women and children,
and was wired with electricity throughout. It had a complete operating theatre and first aid post, independent
water supply from deep springs within the cliff, kitchen,
clothes and bedding space. Also it had sufficient food
storage to feed all shelterers and staff for fourteen days if
necessary. During the days and nights of heavy shelling it
and all the other shelters were full to capacity, and even
now that much of the danger is over, there are still nurses
and other helpers on duty there night and day. 'After all',
one of them said, 'there is still Dunkirk in German hands,
you know and there is always the chance of a V1 or a V2.'
Many homeless townspeople still sleep in the caves and
we noticed many suitcases and rolls of blankets on the
bunks, the property of modern cave-dwellers. Dover is
certainly to be envied the wonderful protection of these
caves and I could not help wishing Londoners had been
able to burrow so deep.

From the caves we drove up to the heights of the
cliff tops and there the Control Officer showed us the
outlook posts manned night and day by wardens who
watch the flash of guns on the French coast. The whole
of the coast line was marked out in sections on a map

and directly the warden spotted a flash, say in section 2Y, he immediately telephoned down to the control centre in the town and rescue workers and ambulances were ready to dash to that part of the town where the shells from that particular gunsite would fall.

In this way confusion was avoided and many lives saved. We talked with one of the outlook wardens on duty – a wonderful old man of 72 – just as keen and virile as a man half his age. He has taken regular duty hours from the beginning and told us he would not change his post for anything in the world. It must have been pretty lonely away up on that cliff top at night with shells falling round or screaming into the town far below – just two men and a telephone in that queer little hut buried up to eye-level in the earth. And yet one could understand his pride.

As we were waiting for our train back to London, the stationmaster said with a grin – 'well we've been through some strange nights and days and we've often wondered just what would happen next – but here we are. Now our one idea is to put everything to rights again as quickly as possible.'

Well – good luck Dover – we hope your troubles are over and that now the big tidy up can begin.

Many people were still in need of a place to live, as well as the most basic items, as Constance Logan-Wright's report of a later visit shows:

29th January 1945
Mrs King and I have been down to one of the Rehabilitation Centres run by the WVS in a district

which has suffered most from rocket bombs recently. Here victims of Hitler's visitations come for clothing and household essentials such as a tin kettle, saucepan, brush, blanket (one of the latter is allowed for each member of a family) and here today, for the first time, some of the cretonne chair covers you gave were being given out. When we arrived there was a long queue of old men, women, and children outside the large temporarily roofed-in hall. Inside were long trestle tables piled with the quota of gifts which were to be handed out today. These gifts were so precious that they have to be very carefully allotted and each recipient has to hand in a card on which has been written official details of damage their home has suffered and their most urgent requirements. For instance only those with a chair or a sofa left would be allowed to take one of the covers – those whose homes have been destroyed and who are living at the Rest Centres would have to wait until they had a home to go to. There was great excitement over some of our Bundles blankets – they were gay lovely things and naturally everyone wanted such a bit of bright colour to cheer up their blitzed home. I was so surprised to see these blankets, knowing that you have not sent any over for many months now – but it was explained that these had been held for emergencies in many parts of Britain and are now being released for all the areas suffering from rocket bombs. They gave the recipients the greatest joy and many recipients had tears in their eyes as they went away. So too with the patchwork quilts made from coloured pieces of flannelette – the brighter the colour the more precious they are because they help so enormously to decorate a dingy paintless room.

Further down the hall were tables covered with china teapots, little vases, jampots, plates, spoons, knives, and forks, bits of looking glass, soap dishes, etc, just about anything one needs when all one's belongings are gone. These things had been sent in by towns and villages in the 'safe' areas of England. Most had already seen good service, but since they are all difficult to buy new, they were eagerly snatched up. Quite a lot of framed pictures, photographs and texts have come in from the same source. Some of the latter we felt had not been very well chosen, one in particular, 'Prepare to meet thy God' was perhaps not the most encouraging text one could select for people who are every day and every hour in the 'firing' line!

Ann Maxtone Graham, who had been living in the relative safety of Market Harborough, returned home to London:

The two houses directly [to the] back of us had been removed by a bomb. The garden wall had fallen in, which made a horrid mess. I had opened up all the windows carefully and thoroughly, and not one bit of glass was broken. The whole window frame in the nursery bathroom had blown loose and hung down from the top, but the glass was intact. The shoring up I had had put up in the basement passageway was removed. We did a little painting and a little wall washing, and then it began to look almost human. I can't remember how I found a builder to do all the odd jobs, but it was a minor miracle, for everybody wanted someone to fix their houses in any way possible. On the workmen's last day I came out of the kitchen (now our living room) with a broom in my hand to speak to the foreman, who was getting ready to depart.

'You know, I'm not very happy about this ceiling,' I said. 'It looks a bit shaky to me.'

'Shaky, Madam, no, sound as a drum,' and he took the broom out of my hands and gave it a good bang with the end of the handle, whereupon the whole thing came down on our heads.

Choc Steed also returned home, to Plymouth. On 3 July 1945, while her husband Roy was in Australia still serving with the Royal Navy, their son Keith was born:

Keith was christened on 31st October in St Andrew's church where Roy and I were married and he behaved very well! Perhaps I should say that he was christened in the ruins of St Andrews as the church was just a shell then, but has since been rebuilt. Roy came home on 25th February 1946 and we were a complete family at last.

The last V-2 to hit Britain came over on 27 March 1945, and the last action of any kind against British civilians occurred two days later when a V-1 landed in Duckworth, Hertfordshire.

Tom King was part of the coastal defences and so was still hard at work even in these last days:

Wednesday 2nd May 1945
Had two months' notice today from CD duties which we finish on July 1st. We seem to have had a good run so I cannot grumble. The part-timers finish altogether from today so it seems the war is over at last. Crowds of planes about all day, still on supplies for Holland, also had

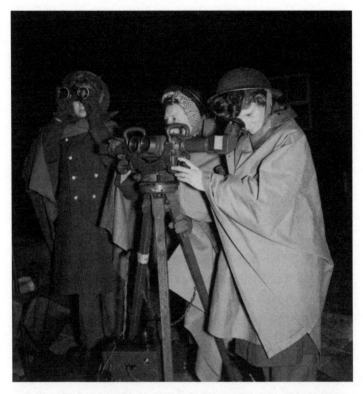

ATS women operate a rangefinder at a 3.7in anti-aircraft gun site firing against V-1 flying bombs, 21 July 1944. The Auxiliary Territorial Service played a major role in Britain's anti-aircraft defences, working on mixed anti-aircraft batteries and searchlights. Efforts by anti-aircraft and the RAF to divert and shoot down V-1s were quite successful, though they had no effect against V-2 rockets, which travelled faster than the speed of sound. *Courtesy of the Imperial War Museum*

notification today that the siren finishes today at 12.00. We have had 2,046 warnings since the war started.

Betty Holbrook's time in the ATS was coming to an end too:

One of the points we brought up was that none of the ATS who had been on the site for two years was entitled to a Defence Medal. We just had not been in uniform the three years necessary to apply for one. We all knew people who had never even HEARD a civilian air raid warning but because they had been in uniform for three years they had got a medal! We remembered that Sir Frederick Pile, the biggest man in ack-ack, had visited the site and told us face to face that the girls on anti-aircraft on operational duties were the cream of the ATS. BUT NO MEDALS FOR US! We had also heard that Sir Freddie was trying to get a special medal for London Anti-Aircraft people. What a hope! So, NO MEDALS FOR US!

A nice memory was of us walking around an open market in the East End of London about the time of the 'Little Blitz' in 1943/44. We were in battledress, with our boots and gaiters on and wearing our sleeveless long leather jerkins; very spick and span with our red anti-aircraft flash on our sleeves plus the special radar flash; a red circle with white 'sparks' coming out of it. It was rather embarrassing, but we got a round of applause from the stallholders and their customers. Some cheered! Some of the male stallholders came out and kissed us on our cheeks and some of the women hugged us. 'Well done, girls!' We grew taller. Probably had tears in our eyes. 'WOW!' we said as we left. That was really something! Maybe they could keep their bloody medals!!!

POSTSCRIPT

Most of those whose experiences feature in this book survived the war; of a few, there is little information beyond the accounts from which we have quoted.

As peace came, the aim of 'getting back to normal' was uppermost in people's minds. Fortunately, many nevertheless kept their letters and diaries and reflected on their experiences years later, writing memoirs of what had been an extraordinary time for all who lived through it.

Ann Maxtone Graham was reunited with her children in 1944, although she wrote that her eldest son Peter resented her for leaving them in America. She and her husband Pat separated in 1946, whereupon she returned with John and Michael, her twin sons, to the USA; Peter, after service in the navy, went east to become a tea planter.

Of the doctors who wrote about working through air raids, John Lee enjoyed several years of retirement. Sadly, Wilfred Willway, who knew he was terminally ill when he published his observations, died in 1944, aged 36.

When Phil Piratin wrote his memoirs, in 1948, he was MP for Mile End in Stepney. Another MP, Duff Cooper, became, briefly, Minister of Information in Churchill's cabinet and ended the war as Britain's ambassador in Paris.

J. Grenville Atherton, Harry Atterbury, Mary Baker, Cecil Beaton, Elizabeth and John Belsey, Vera Brittain, Roy Clevely, Pam Cleverley, Phillip Chignell, Alan Deere, James Doherty, Leslie Gardiner, Kathleen Hanlon, Betty Holbrook, Mary Haggerty, Tom King, Claire Lowry, Anne Lee Michell, Joyce Pomorska, Choc Steed, Donald Thompson, Ilie Wilson, R.H. Lloyd-Jones and Muriel Simkin survived for years after the war.

Intriguingly, Betty Bullard's diary ends in 1945 just as she is about to go to India with the ATS; she is wondering if Peter, her boyfriend of several years, will join her there and whether he will propose to her.

The most extraordinary tale is that of Henry Beckingham. He survived the entire conflict working in bomb disposal, and by May 1945 was in charge of clearing mines in the Channel Islands, where he remained until 1946. He ended his military career as a captain and was last heard of enjoying a long retirement, having published several books.

Appendix One

ABBREVIATIONS

AA	Anti-Aircraft
ACW	Aircraftwoman
AFS	Auxiliary Fire Service
ARP	Air Raid Precautions
ATS	Auxiliary Territorial Service
CD	Civil Defence
EMS	Emergency Medical Service
GPO	General Post Office
HE	High Explosive
HQ	Headquarters
LFB	London Fire Brigade
ME	Messerschmitt
MO	Medical Officer
MTC	Mechanised Transport Corps
NFS	National Fire Service

RAF	Royal Air Force
ROC	Royal Observer Corps
UXB	Unexploded bomb
WAAF	Women's Auxiliary Air Force
WAFS	Women's Auxiliary Fire Service
WVS	Women's Voluntary Service

TIMELINE

1 January 1938
ARP Act means local authorities must organise Air Raid
Precautions.

September 1938
Munich Crisis: war seems imminent. Adds impetus to ARP
and gasmask distribution.

1 September 1939
Germany invades Poland.

3 September 1939
Britain declares war on Germany.

Spring 1940
Luftwaffe attacks on fighter squadron airfields.

Spring 1940
First UK civilian deaths from aerial action, in Orkney and in Clacton-on-Sea.

26 June – 16 July 1940
Luftwaffe launches scattered attacks and mine-laying sorties, mainly against ports and shipping in the English Channel, and towns with factories supplying the war effort.

17 July – 12 August 1940
Increasing and larger daylight attacks over Britain against shipping; ports along south and east coasts, and some coastal airfields. Increased night attacks against the west, the Midlands, and east coast, RAF bases, as well as armaments and aircraft factories.

15 August 1940
Croydon bombed by Luftwaffe.

August 1940 – May 1941
Liverpool Blitz. After London, Liverpool is the UK's most heavily bombed city.

25 August 1940
Tempelshof suburb of Berlin bombed by the RAF.

5 September 1940
Hitler says Germany will avenge Tempelshof.

7 September 1940

First German raid over central London, marking the start of the Blitz. London is the target for raids for the next fifty-seven nights, except for one night of bad weather.

17 September 1940

Hitler postpones plans to invade Britain. Blitz continues as a diversion while Germany prepares for attack on Russia.

14 November 1940

First raid on Coventry. Subsequently, raids on major towns and cities give some respite to London.

22–24 December 1940

Manchester suffers its heaviest raids.

29 December 1940

Second Great Fire of London. Docks and central areas of London set blaze in the heaviest night of bombing over Greater London so far.

31 December 1940

Government announces fire-watching scheme to tackle incendiary bombs.

Early 1941

British ports, especially in the south west and west, attacked as Luftwaffe adds its weight to the Battle of the Atlantic.

13–15 March 1941

Clydebank Blitz.

7 April – 5 May 1941
Belfast Blitz.

16 and 19 April 1941
The 'Wednesday Raid' and the 'Saturday Raid' – two major raids over London, possibly in retaliation for heavy raids by RAF on Berlin.

10 May 1941
Last and heaviest major bombing raid on London. End of the Big Blitz.

22 June 1941
Hitler invades Russia. Air raids over Britain scaled back as Luftwaffe concentrates its resources on attacking Russia.

September 1941
National Fire Service announced, to co-ordinate brigades across the country.

6 August 1941
Fire Guard formed, expanding the firewatching scheme.

28 March 1942
RAF attacks medieval town of Lübeck.

April 1942
Start of the Baedeker Raids.
Luftwaffe attacks historic British cities and towns in retaliation for Lübeck.

June 1943
First anti-personnel 'butterfly' bombs dropped over UK.

January – May 1944
Operation Steinbock, also known as the Little Blitz and the Baby Blitz.

13 June 1944
First V-1 attack.

8 September 1944
First V-2 attack.

27 March 1945
Last V-2 attack.

29 March 1945
Last V-1 attack.

8 May 1945
Germany surrenders.

Appendix Three

AIR RAID CASUALTIES

146,777 civilians were killed, missing believed killed, or seriously injured, subdivided as follows:

Men: 67,661
Women: 63,221
Children under 16: 15,358
Unidentified: 537

Civil defence workers on duty (the General Services and the Regular and Auxiliary Police and Fire Services) suffered 6,838 casualties (2,379 killed and 4,459 seriously injured), which are included in the previous total. Of these, 6,220 were men and 618 women.

The proportion of casualties attributed to the enemy's chief weapons has been estimated as follows:

	Killed	Seriously Injured	Total
Bombs	51,509	61,423	112,932
Flying bombs	6,184	17,981	24,165
Long-range rockets	2,754	6,523	9,277
Cross-Channel bombardment	148	255	403
Total	60,595	86,182	146,777

London suffered over 80,000 of the estimated total for the country of 146,777 fatal and serious casualties. Outside London, only Birmingham and Liverpool suffered more than 5,000 such casualties.

Major bombardments (attacks in which more than 100 tons of HE bombs were successfully aimed at the target):

London	71
Birmingham	8
Liverpool, Birkenhead	8
Plymouth-Devonport	8
Bristol-Avonmouth	6
Glasgow-Clydeside	5
Southampton	4
Hull	3
Manchester	3
Portsmouth	3
Belfast	2
Coventry	2
Cardiff	1
Newcastle-Tyneside	1
Nottingham	1
Sheffield	1

FLYING BOMB AND LONG-RANGE ROCKET
INCIDENTS BY COUNTY

Counties	Flying Bombs	Long-Range Rockets
London (region)	2,420	517
Kent	1,444	64
Sussex	886	4
Essex	412	378
Surrey	295	8
Suffolk	93	13
Hertfordshire	82	34
Hampshire	80	–
Buckinghamshire	27	2
Norfolk	13	29
Berkshire	12	1
Bedfordshire	10	3
Lancashire	8	–
Yorkshire	7	–
Cheshire	6	–
Cambridgeshire	5	1
Northamptonshire	4	–
Oxfordshire	4	–
Isle of Ely	3	–
Derbyshire	3	–
Huntingdonshire	2	–
Lincolnshire	2	–
Durham	1	–
Nottinghamshire	1	–
Leicestershire	1	–
Rutland	1	–
Shropshire	1	–
Total	**5,823★**	**1,054†**

★ London Region received 41 per cent of flying bombs and 49 per cent of long-range rockets; † 271 of these flying bombs and 4 of the long-range rockets fell in the sea.
From: *Civil Defence* T.H. O'Brian

ACKNOWLEDGEMENTS

We are grateful to many people who have helped us with personal memories and diaries during the research for this project, and especially those in family history and local history societies and archives.

Thanks are due to Alex Waite, Amy Rigg, Sophie Bradshaw, Abigail Wood, and Christine McMorris from The History Press, and the staff of the Research Room at the Imperial War Museum.

Thanks too to William and Ralph Harris-Brown for their administrative support, and, as ever, their patience.

We are grateful too to the following for their kind permission to quote from original material: Gill Ankers for the letter of her mother, Kathleen Hanlon; Fiona Godlee, editor-in-chief of the *British Medical Journal*, for permission to reproduce the letter from Dr Duncan Leys and extracts from papers by Robert Lee and F. Wilfred Willway; Glasgow City Council archives for memories of James Hastings and Tryphena Nixon.

Thanks also to the many individual contributors and their families for allowing us to use the following original documents: J.G. Atherton, H.W. Atterbury, C.M. Baker, Henry Beckingham, Elizabeth Belsey, John Belsey, C. Brownbill, Betty Bullard, Margaret Chifney, Phillip Chignell, Roy Clevely, H.R. Clothier, Betty Holbrook, Kenneth Holmes, Constance Logan-Wright, Claire Lowry, Tom King, Anne Lee Michell, R.H. Lloyd-Jones, Hetty Long, Ann Maxtone Graham, Lily Pearson, Joyce Pomorska, Choc Steed, J.L. Stevens, Don Thompson, Jeanne and Marion Thompson, Rose Uttin and Mollie Wilson.

We are also grateful to Graeme Kirkwood, historian for Strathclyde fire services, for the report by A.S. Pratten; Jim Purdey for his private memoir; West Glamorgan Archive Service for permission to quote from the diary of Basil Radford; the Museum of London for permission to reproduce the letter from Will, the ARP warden in Leytonstone, Bob Boyd, John Simkin of Spartacus Educational, and to Frank Chalmers for the loan of *Our Flag Stays Red*.

SOURCES AND FURTHER READING

Aylmer Firebrace, Commander Sir, *Fire Service Memories*, Andrew Melrose, 1948

Barry Hollis, *The Forgotten Front Line*, Enthusiasts Publications, 1985

Bob Boyd, *The Day War Broke Out*, Bromley U3As, 1995

Carol Harris, *Women at War 1939-45: The Home Front*, The History Press, 2000

Cecil Beaton, *The Years Between: Diaries 1939–44*, Weidenfeld & Nicolson, 1965

Eric Wilton, *Centre Crew: A Memory of the Royal Observer Corps*, published privately, 1946

Frederick Pile, Gen. Sir, *Ack-Ack*, George G. Harrap, 1949

James Doherty, *Post 381*, Friar's Bush Press, 1989

Mike Brown, *Put That Light Out*, Sutton, 1999

Muriel Simkin, ed. John Simkin, *Voices From the Past: The Blitz*, Spartacus, 1987

N.W. Hardy, *Eastbourne 1939–45: A Complete Record of Nearly Six Years of War in Eastbourne*, Strange the Printer Ltd, 1945

Peter Chrisp, *The Blitz: Mass Observation Teaching Booklet No. 1*, University of Sussex Library, 1987

Phil Piratin, *Our Flag Stays Red*, Thames Publications, 1948

Quentin Reynolds, *The Wounded Don't Cry*, E.P. Dutton, 1941

Reginald Bell, *The London Bullseye*, Cassell and Co., 1943

Terrence O'Brien, *Civil Defence*, HMSO, 1955

W.L. Richards, *Pembrokeshire Under Fire: The Story of the Air Raids of 1940–41*, J.W. Hammond and Co. Ltd, 1965

William Sansom, *Westminster in War*, Faber & Faber, 1947